A Parent's Guide to the Common Core

Grade 6

© 2014 Kaplan, Inc.

Published by Kaplan Publishing, a division of Kaplan, Inc.
395 Hudson Street
New York, NY 10014

Printed in the United States of America

10 9 8 7 6 5 4 3 2 1

ISBN-13: 978-1-61865-819-7

Kaplan Publishing books are available at special quantity discounts to use for sales promotions, employee premiums, or educational purposes. For more information or to purchase books, please call the Simon & Schuster special sales department at 866-506-1949.

TABLE OF CONTENTS

INTRODUCTION TO THE COMMON CORE STANDARDS

This book is designed to introduce you and your child to the Common Core Standards, a major development in the way U.S. students are taught the most basic and critical areas of knowledge that they will encounter while in school. The Common Core Standards will be used to create assessments beginning in the 2014-2015 school year.

Where did the Common Core Standards come from?

The Common Core Standards were developed to create more uniform academic standards across the United States. Since each state has traditionally created its own academic standards and assessments, students in one state would often end up studying different things than students in another state. Education professionals from across the nation worked together to select the best and most relevant standards from all the states, and then used these as the basis for new standards that could be used by every state to ensure that all students are fully prepared for the future. The Common Core Standards are, in many cases, more comprehensive and demanding than previous state standards. These new standards are designed to help American students perform favorably against students from other developed nations—an area in which the United States has fallen behind in recent years.

The Common Core Standards were not created by the federal government. Each state may choose whether it wishes to use the Common Core Standards, or stick with its own unique learning standards. However, most states have recognized the importance of consistent and high-level standards for all American students. At printing, forty-five states, along with the District of Columbia and four U.S. territories, have adopted the Common Core Standards.

What are the Common Core Standards?

The Common Core Standards are the standards to which all students will be held. These standards are applicable for grades K-12. The Common Core Standards focus on two areas of learning: English Language Arts and Mathematics. These areas were chosen because they are critical to developing a solid foundation for learning, and encompass other fields such as social studies and science.

Within English Language Arts, the Common Core Standards are divided into several categories: Reading; Writing; Speaking & Listening; and Language. For Grade 6, reading standards are focused on evaluating the validity of arguments and conveying ideas without bias, as well as describing plot and character progression in reading passages. Writing standards focus on developing arguments that are supported by credible and relevant evidence and organized in a logical way. These skills are critical for building a foundation for success, both in school and in later life.

Within Mathematics, the Common Core Standards are also divided into several categories. For Grade 6, these categories are: Ratios & Proportional Relationships; The Number System; Expressions & Equations; Geometry; and Statistics & Probability. For Grade 6, Ratios & Proportional Relationships focuses mainly on understanding ratios and rates between two quantities, and expressing ratios in terms of percentage. The Number System focuses on dividing fractions and graphing on a coordinate plane. Expressions & Equations focuses on using variables to solve basic equations. These skills have been identified as critical for success in other areas such as the sciences.

The Common Core Standards do not dictate a teacher's curriculum; they just ensure that all teachers are working toward the same learning standards. Teachers were instrumental in developing the standards, and remain the dominant force in helping your child achieve academic potential. However, as a parent, you now have the opportunity to see the "road map" that your child's teachers will be using to build their courses of study. This allows you to better become an active participant in helping your child achieve these learning goals.

How to use this book

This book is designed to provide you with the tools necessary to help your child succeed. While the Common Core Standards are numerous for each grade level, Kaplan's learning experts have identified the standards that are most critical for success, both in the classroom and on assessment tests. These are known as the "power standards." Each lesson in this book is dedicated to a different power standard. The power standards are also the focus of the tests and quizzes throughout the book.

You should begin by having your child take the Pre-Test for each domain. The Pre-Test is designed to cover the same skills that will likely be tested on state assessments. This will give you an idea of the areas in which your child excels, as well as the areas that may need special attention.

Once you have gauged your child's baseline skills, the lessons offer practical experience with each of the power standards. Each lesson provides information on what the standard means, and offers examples of how the standard might be addressed through classroom teaching and through testing. In addition, each lesson offers an activity that you can engage in with your child to help practice the skills highlighted in the lesson. Once you are confident in your child's abilities with regard to a lesson, you can have your child take the end-of-lesson quiz for that power standard to ensure mastery.

When you have completed all the lessons, have your child complete the Post-Test for each domain. You can compare your child's performance on the Post-Test to the Pre-Test, and see which areas have improved the most. If some areas still need work, re-read the corresponding lesson with your child, and try to pinpoint the specific issue that your child needs additional help mastering. The List of Resources provided with this book includes a number of Web sites, publications, and other types of resources that can help you and your child continue to practice and reinforce the Common Core Standards.

Common Core State Standards Initiative: http://www.corestandards.org/.
This Web site offers in-depth information about the Common Core Standards and their history.

National Library of Virtual Manipulatives: http://nlvm.usu.edu/en/nav/vlibrary.html.
This National Science Foundation supported project allows students, teachers, and parents to interact with virtual manipulatives that can aid in teaching basic mathematic principles.

Math Videos by Math Playground: http://www.mathplayground.com/mathvideos.html.
These videos address a wide range of math-related questions, from "How do you add fractions?" to "How do you solve an inequality?"

Inside Mathematics: http://www.insidemathematics.org/.
This invaluable resource, intended primarily for educators, includes tools for teaching math as well as a section addressing the Common Core Standards.

New Common Core Math Problems and Resources: https://www.khanacademy.org/commoncore.
Khan Academy, one of the world's premier not-for-profit online classrooms, offers practice problems that are mapped to the specific Common Core Standards and organized by grade level.

Illustrative Mathematics: http://www.illustrativemathematics.org/6.
This site offers examples to illustrate the Common Core Standards for every grade level.

Free Activities and Worksheets from Flashkids: http://www.flashkids.com/free-downloads.
These activities and worksheets are broken down by domain and grade level, and can be a fun way to improve skills critical to Common Core.

Parents' Guide to Student Success, 6th Grade: http://pta.org/files/6th_Grade__BW.pdf.
This overview from the National Parent-Teacher Association tells you in detail what you should expect from a curriculum aimed at meeting Common Core Standards.

Parent Roadmaps to the Common Core Standards—English Language Arts: http://www.cgcs.org/Domain/36.
The Council of the Great City Schools offers parent roadmaps to help you support your child in math and English language arts at each grade level.

Working with the "Shifts": http://www.engageny.org/sites/default/files/resource/attachments/parent_workshop_what_parents_can_do_handout.pdf.

This handout from the New York State Education Department explains in detail how the Common Core Standards have shifted the content and methods used by teachers, and offers suggestions for how you can help your student thrive amid these changes.

Achieve the Core: http://www.achievethecore.org/.
This Web site was created by the main creators of the Common Core Standards as a way to provide free teaching materials tailored to help students master the skills needed to meet these standards.

ReadWriteThink Tips & How-To Resources for Parents: http://www.readwritethink.org/search/?grade=8-12&resource_type=74.
This site, supported by the International Reading Association and the National Council of Teachers of English, provides tips to help parents nurture their child's interest in reading and the language arts.

PBS Parents: Reading & Language: http://www.pbs.org/parents/education/reading-language/.
This Web site, affiliated with the Public Broadcasting Service (PBS), offers advice for improving your child's literacy and love of reading.

The Adventures of Tom Sawyer **by Mark Twain.**
This classic children's novel, available in the public domain, is an excellent text for sixth-grade readers. It is considered a prime example of the type of text used to test Common Core Standards at the sixth-grade level.

Little Women **by Louisa May Alcott.**
Another classic novel available in the public domain, this is considered a prime example of the type of text used to test sixth-grade Common Core Standards.

American Library Association Summer Reading List, Grades 6-8: http://www.ala.org/alsc/sites/ala.org.alsc/files/content/SummerReadingList_6-8_Color.pdf.
This list, aimed and keeping kids involved in reading during their summer months, includes titles that are highly recommended by student readers at the same grade level as your child.

ENGLISH LANGUAGE ARTS PRE-TEST

The pre-test is intended as a preliminary assessment of your child's language arts skills. The questions cover reading comprehension, vocabulary, and writing. There are a variety of question types at various levels of cognition. These are typical of the types of questions that your sixth grader might experience in the classroom, as homework, and in assessment situations.

A grid at the end provides the main Common Core standard assessed, as well as a brief explanation of the correct answers. This is intended to provide information about which standards your child might need the most help with. Because of this, you may want to encourage your child to take an educated guess on questions that he or she is unsure of, but to mark these with a question mark. This will help you identify areas that might need reinforcement.

The items on the pre-test are not designed to replicate standardized tests used to assess a child's reading level or a school's progress in helping the child achieve grade level.

Read the following two paragraphs aloud to your child:

This test includes questions to test reading, vocabulary, and writing skills. Please answer as best as possible. The test will not be graded. If you come across a question that you are unsure of, put a question mark next to it and make your best guess.

Some of the questions are based on stories or other reading passages. Read the passage carefully. If you don't know the answer to a question, look back at the passage to see if you can find it.

Directions: For each section, read the passage and then answer the questions that follow.

 Tsunamis

Some people like to sit on a beach and watch the waves crash on the rocks or the shoreline. Others love to surf the high-pounding waves. But everyone fears a truly huge wave—a wall of water that can be more than eighty feet high and can destroy an entire coastal town.

These huge waves are called tsunamis. *Tsunami* is a Japanese word that means "storm wave." They have also been called "tidal waves." But they are not caused by tides. Most are caused by earthquakes that occur under the sea. Some have occurred during the eruption of an underwater volcano or because of a hurricane. Earthquakes happen near cracks, or faults, that lie near the surface of the earth. If underground movement makes the rocks shift near a fault, an earthquake will occur. When a fault moves back and forth on the ocean floor, a tsunami will *not* be formed. But if the fault moves up and down, ripples of water will move rapidly on the ocean's surface and result in a tsunami. These ripples can move at 400 to 500 miles per hour. The waves themselves are usually only about a yard high. But by the time the tsunami hits the shore, it has grown to an enormous height and can be very destructive.

Most tsunamis occur in the Pacific Ocean. This is because it has many earthquakes and volcanoes. The greatest number of tsunamis happen in Japan, Hawaii, Alaska, and on the west coast of the United States.

Fortunately, scientists can often predict when a giant wave will occur. After an earthquake, they can calculate how long it will take the tsunami to travel across the ocean to hit a particular coast. The speed of a tsunami depends on how deep the water is in that stretch of ocean.

1. In the first paragraph, why does the author make the statement that "everyone fears a truly huge wave"?
    A. to show how some people love surfing
    B. to introduce the idea that tsunamis are dangerous
    C. to make a serious subject seem humorous
    D. to describe the author's own fears of tsunamis

2. What happens if a fault moves up and down after an earthquake?
    A. A tsunami is formed.
    B. The tsunami grows taller.
    C. The tsunami stops growing.
    D. A crack forms in the ocean floor.

3. Most tsunamis occur in the Pacific Ocean because
    A. the water is warm.
    B. it is the largest ocean.
    C. there are many islands there.
    D. there are many volcanoes there.

4. Based on its usage in the second paragraph, which of the following is closest in meaning to the word *eruption*?
    A. hole   B. explosion   C. emergency   D. crash

5. What determines the speed of a tsunami?

_____

6. What causes earthquakes in the ocean?
    A. the density of the ocean water
    B. faults moving back and forth
    C. underground movement near a fault
    D. the presence of an underwater volcano

7. Based on its usage in the last paragraph, which of the following is closest in meaning to the word *calculate*?

A. *guess*   B. *prevent*   C. *warn*   D. *estimate*

Excerpt from *Rebecca of Sunnybrook Farm* by Kate Douglas Wiggin

The old stage coach was rumbling along the dusty road that runs from Maplewood to Riverboro. The day was as warm as midsummer, though it was only the middle of May, and Mr. Jeremiah Cobb was favoring the horses as much as possible, yet never losing sight of the fact that he carried the mail. The hills were many, and the reins lay loosely in his hands as he lolled back in his seat and extended one foot and leg luxuriously over the dashboard. His brimmed hat of worn felt was well pulled over his eyes, and he revolved a quid of tobacco in his left cheek.

There was one passenger in the coach, -- a small dark-haired person in a glossy buff calico dress. She was so slender and so stiffly starched that she slid from space to space on the leather cushions, though she braced herself against the middle seat with her feet and extended her cotton-gloved hands on each side, in order to maintain some sort of balance. Whenever the wheels sank farther than usual into a rut, or jolted suddenly over a stone, she bounded involuntarily into the air, came down again, pushed back her funny little straw hat, and picked up or settled more firmly a small pink sun shade, which seemed to be her chief responsibility, -- unless we except a bead purse, into which she looked whenever the condition of the roads would permit, finding great apparent satisfaction in that its precious contents neither disappeared nor grew less. Mr. Cobb guessed nothing of these harassing details of travel, his business being to carry people to their destinations, not, necessarily, to make them comfortable on the way. Indeed he had forgotten the very existence of this one unnoteworthy little passenger.

When he was about to leave the post-office in Maplewood that morning, a woman had alighted from a wagon, and coming up to him, inquired whether this were the Riverboro stage, and if he were Mr. Cobb. Being answered in the affirmative, she nodded to a child who was eagerly waiting for the answer, and who ran towards her as if she feared to be a moment too late. The child might have been ten or eleven years old perhaps, but whatever the number of her summers, she had an air of being small for her age. Her mother helped her into the stage coach, deposited a bundle and a bouquet of lilacs beside her, superintended the "roping on" behind of an old hair trunk, and finally paid the fare, counting out the silver with great care.

"I want you should take her to my sisters' in Riverboro," she said. "Do you know Mirandy and Jane Sawyer? They live in the brick house."

Lord bless your soul, he knew 'em as well as if he'd made 'em!

"Well, she's going there, and they're expecting her. Will you keep an eye on her, please? If she can get out anywhere and get with folks, or get anybody in to keep her company, she'll do it. Good-by, Rebecca; try not to get into any mischief, and sit quiet, so you'll look neat an' nice when you get there. Don't be any trouble to Mr. Cobb. -- You see, she's kind of excited. -- We came on the cars from Temperance yesterday, slept all night at my cousin's, and drove from her house -- eight miles it is -- this morning."

8. Which sentence from the passage best tells why Rebecca was not comfortable inside the coach?

    A. *"She was so slender that she slid from space to space on the leather cushions inside the coach, even though she braced herself by putting her feet on the seat in front of her and placing her cotton-gloved hands on each side."*

    B. *"The child might have been ten or eleven years old perhaps, but whatever the number of her summers, she had an air of being small for her age."*

    C. *"There was one passenger in the coach, -- a small dark-haired person in a glossy buff calico dress."*

    D. *"The hills were many, and the reins lay loosely in his hands as he lolled back in his seat and extended one foot and leg luxuriously over the dashboard."*

9. How does Rebecca's mother describe Rebecca to the stage coach driver?

    A. *timid and shy*   B. *moody and grumpy*

    C. *nervous and worried*   D. *excited and mischievous*

10. Based on its usage in the first paragraph, which of the following is the closest in meaning to the word *quid*?

    A. *very*   B. *portion*   C. *foursome*   D. *rapid*

11. Based on the words and actions of the characters, which of the following can you infer about Rebecca?

    A. *she is very frightened of horses*

    B. *the purpose of her journey is to give some bad news to her relatives*

    C. *she is a frequent traveler accustomed to style and comfort*

    D. *this is her first time traveling such a long distance*

12. Based on its usage in the second paragraph, which of the following is closest in meaning to the word *unnoteworthy*?

    A. *important*   B. *mischievous*   C. *unremarkable*   D. *unattractive*

13. According to the passage, where is Rebecca traveling to?

    A. *Sunnybrook Farm*   B. *Maplewood*

    C. *Riverboro*   D. *Temperance*

14. How would you describe Mr. Cobb's attitude toward Rebecca? Use details from the passage in your answer.

_____

_____

_____

_____

15. Write a brief summary of the passage.

_____

_____

_____

_____

Excerpt from "The Arabian Nights: Ali Baba and the Forty Thieves" by Antoine Galland (translated by Edward William Lane, revised by Stanley Lane-Poole)

One day, when Ali Baba was in the forest, and had just cut wood enough to load his donkeys, he saw at a distance a great cloud of dust approaching him. He observed it with attention, and distinguished soon after a body of horsemen, whom he suspected to be robbers. He determined to leave his donkeys in order to save himself; so climbed up a large tree, planted on a high rock, the branches of which were thick enough to conceal him, and yet enabled him to see all that passed without being discovered.

The troop, to the number of forty, well mounted and armed, came to the foot of the rock on which the tree stood, and there dismounted. Every man unbridled his horse, tied him to some shrub, and hung about his neck a bag of corn which they carried behind them. Then each took off his saddle-bag, which from its weight seemed to Ali Baba to be full of gold and silver. One, whom he took to be their captain, came under the tree in which he was concealed, and making his way through some shrubs, pronounced the words: "Open, Simsim!" A door opened in the rock; and after he had made all his troop enter before him, he followed them, when the door shut again of itself.

The robbers stayed some time within the rock, during which Ali Baba, fearful of being caught, remained in the tree.

At last the door opened again, and as the captain went in last, so he came out first, and stood to see them all pass by him; when Ali Baba heard him make the door close by pronouncing the words: "Shut, Simsim!" Every man at once went and bridled his horse, fastened his wallet, and mounted again; and when the captain saw them all ready, he put himself at their head, and returned the way they had come.

Ali Baba followed them with his eyes as far as he could see them, and afterward waited a long time before he descended. Remembering the words the captain of the robbers used to cause the door to open and shut, he wished to try if his pronouncing them would have the same effect. Accordingly he went among the shrubs, and, receiving the door concealed behind them, stood before it, and said, "Open, Simsim" Whereupon the door instantly flew wide open.

Now Ali Baba expected a dark, dismal cavern, but was surprised to see a well-lighted and spacious chamber, lighted from an opening at the top of the rock, and filled with all sorts of provisions, rich bales of silk, embroideries, and valuable tissues, piled upon one another, gold and silver ingots in great heaps, and money in bags. The sight of all these riches made him suppose that this cave must have been occupied for ages by robbers, who had succeeded one another.

Ali Baba went boldly into the cave, and collected as much of the gold coin, which was in bags, as his three donkeys could carry. When he had loaded them with the bags, he laid wood over them so that they could not be seen. Then he stood before the door, and pronouncing the words, "Shut, Simsim!" the door closed of itself; and he made the best of his way to the town.

When he got home, he drove his donkeys into a little yard, shut the gates carefully, threw off the wood that covered the panniers, carried the bags into his house, and ranged them in order before his wife. He then emptied the bags, which raised such a heap of gold as dazzled his wife's eyes, and then he told her the whole adventure from beginning to end, and, above all, recommended her to keep it secret.

16. Why does Ali Baba climb up into a tree?
    A. He was warmer in the trees.
    B. An animal was chasing him.
    C. He was scared of the robbers.
    D. He wanted the robbers to see him.

17. Ali Baba tells his wife to keep silent about the gold because
    A. the gold is not real.
    B. the robbers were nearby.
    C. he thought it would be safer.
    D. he wanted to surprise his friends.

18. Based on its usage in the passage, which of the following words is closest in meaning to *dismal*?
    A. gloomy   B. hopeless   C. disgusting   D. remote

19. Based on this excerpt of the story, do you think that Ali Baba is a greedy man? Support your opinion with evidence.

    _____

    _____

20. Write a summary of the story. Be sure to include the most important events.

    _____

    _____

    _____

    _____

Read the paragraph and decide on the best answer to fill each blank.

(1) I _____ try out for the school play, but that would mean giving up my clarinet lessons for a few weeks. (2) My parents _____ very keen on the idea. (3) They _____ I should stick with the clarinet. (4) Then I _____ for the school band starting in the fall. (5) In the end, I solved the problem by not _____ for the school play!

21. In sentence 1, which is the best choice to fill the blank?
    A. didn't want to   B. wanted to   C. couldn't   D. can't

22. In sentence 2, which is the best choice to fill the blank?
    A. weren't   B. aren't   C. were   D. are

23. In sentence 3, which is the best choice to fill the blank?
    A. *have been thinking*   B. *will think*
    C. *thought*   D. *have thought*

24. In sentence 4, which is the best choice to fill the blank?
    A. *will have prepared*   B. *would be prepared*
    C. *am prepared*   D. *am preparing*

25. In sentence 5, which is the best choice to fill the blank?
    A. *am choosing*   B. *having chosen*
    C. *choosing*   D. *being chosen*

26. Read this draft of a paragraph. Correct the grammar, punctuation, spelling, and capitalization. Also add a concluding sentence that sums up the argument.

    Many people feel that children should not have cell phones others argue that children should have them for safety purpose's. As a young person, I can see both sides of the arguement. However, Im inclined to think that haveing a cell phone is more positive then negative. For safety reasons, cell phones make a lot of sense. parents can make sure their children use they're phones only for emergency situations. Another reason for kids to have cell phones is that they are the wave of the Future. Just about everyone have one!

    _____

    _____

    _____

    _____

 **Answer Key**

Note: The answers to open-ended, constructed response questions are sample answers. Answers will vary, but look for the main ideas to be included.

Highlight any questions that your child gets wrong. Looking at the wrong answers may help to reveal one or more standards with which your child is struggling. Even if your child has done well on this pretest, reviewing the lessons will help him or her become a better reader and writer.

Passage	Question	Answer	Standard(s)
Tsunamis	1	B	RI.6.8
	2	A	RI.6.1, RI.6.2
	3	D	RI.6.1
	4	B	RI.6.4

Passage	Question	Answer	Standard(s)
	5	The speed of a tsunami is determined by depth of the water where the tsunami is.	RI.6.1
	6	C	RI.6.1
	7	D	RI.6.4
Rebecca of Sunnybrook Farm	8	A	RL.6.1
	9	D	RL.6.1
	10	B	RL.6.4
	11	D	RL.6.3
	12	C	RL.6.4
	13	C	RL.6.1
	14	Mr. Cobb doesn't think very much of Rebecca. In fact, he forgets all about her. His focus is on his horses and on delivering the mail.	RL.6.3
	15	The coachman Mr. Cobb picks up a passenger, a young girl whose mother has arranged to have the girl visit her aunts in Riverboro. Mr. Cobb takes little notice of the girl, who has trouble keeping from bouncing around the inside of the coach during the trip.	RL.6.2
Ali Baba and the Forty Thieves	16	C	RL.6.1
	17	C	RL.6.1, RL.6.3
	18	A	RL.6.4
	19	Answer may vary. Some students may say that since Ali Baba immediately enters the cave and makes off with the gold, he is greedy. Others may say that since this is only part of the story, it's too hard to tell. For example, Ali Baba may be very poor, which might make us say that he isn't greedy.	RL.6.1, W.6.1
	20	Ali Baba is a man who, by chance, sees robbers opening a cave by saying "Open sesame." He then does the same thing and sees the riches in the cave. He gets as much of the gold as he can carry and brings it home. He tells his wife not to say anything about the gold.	RL.6.2
	21	B	W.6.5
	22	A	W.6.5
	23	C	W.6.5
	24	B	W.6.5
	25	D	W.6.5
	26	Many people feel that children should not have cell phones. Others argue that children should have them for safety purposes. As a young person, I can see both sides of the argument. However, I'm inclined to think that having a cell phone is more positive than negative. For safety reasons, cell phones make a lot of sense. Parents can make sure their children use their phones only for emergency situations. Another reason for kids to have cell phones is that they are the wave of the future. Just about everyone has one! In my opinion, children should be given cell phones.	W.6.1, W.6.5

MATHEMATICS PRE-TEST

1. Which is $\dfrac{2}{3} \div \dfrac{3}{8}$?

   A. $\dfrac{1}{4}$ B. $\dfrac{9}{16}$ C. $1\dfrac{7}{9}$ D. 4

2. Adrienne has 12 classical music CDs. This is 40% of all of her CDs. How many CDs does she have? Justify your answer using a double number line diagram.

3. In a pet store, there are 2 cats for every 5 dogs. Which is the correct ratio of dogs to cats in the pet store?

   A. 2:5   B. 2:7   C. 5:2   D. 5:7

4. At a fruit stand, apples sell for $3.60 per dozen. Selena buys 18 apples. How much does she pay?

   A. $3.60   B. $5.40   C. $7.20   D. $9.00

5. On a cereal box label, Karen reads that there are 6 grams of sugar in a 30-gram serving of cereal. What is the percentage of sugar in the serving by weight?

   A. 10 %   B. 20 %   C. 50 %   D. 67 %

Use the coordinate plane to answer questions 6-7.

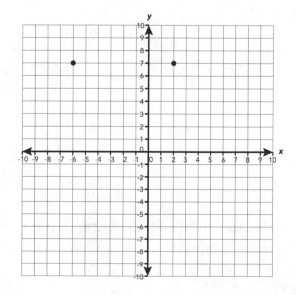

6. What are the coordinates of the two points shown on the coordinate plane?

   A. (2, 7) and (7, –6)   B. (7, 2) and (7, –6)
   C. (2, 7) and (–6, 7)   D. (7, –6) and (2, 2)

7. What is the distance between the two points?

   A. 1 unit   B. 5 units   C. 8 units   D. 13 units

8. A company charges a tax for purchasing a book online. The cost of the book was $15 and the total bill was $16.05. Which equation could you solve to find the dollar amount of the tax?

   A. $15t = 16.05$ B. $16.05t = 15$ C. $t - 16.05 = 15$ D. $t + 15 = 16.05$

9. For the equation $3x + 14 = -1$, the possible solutions are –16, –12, –5, and 5. Which is the correct solution?

   A. –16   B. –12   C. –5   D. 5

10. George travels 1 mile for every 20 minutes that he walks. He walks a total of 6 miles. If he kept a constant pace, how long did he walk? Use the table to solve the problem.

Miles	1	2	3	4	5	6
Minutes	20					

11. If Jim has three times the amount of money as Tina, and both children have a combined total of $12, how much money does Tina have?

   A. $3   B. $4   C. $9   D. $12

12. Sonya weighs 35 kilograms. There are about 2.2 pounds in one kilogram. About how many pounds does Sonya weigh?

   A. 37.2   B. 72   C. 77   D. 89.2

13. Janelle is making chili. She uses this table to show how much salt to use.

Number of Servings	Salt (teaspoons)
1	3
2	6
3	9
4	12

   If t represents the total number of teaspoons of salt needed and c represents the number of servings of chili, which equation shows the relationship between t and c?

   A. $t = c + 3$ B. $c = t + 3$ C. $t - 3c$ D. $c = 3t$

14. What is the ratio of cranberry juice to grape juice shown on the graph below?

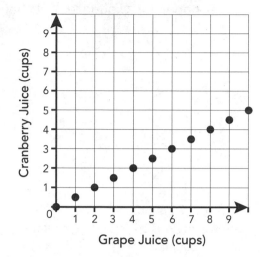

A. 1:4

B. 1:2

C. 2:1

D. 4:1

15. It takes Kim 45 minutes to complete the homework in two of her college courses. If Kim takes 6 courses and she spends the same amount of time on each course, how long will it take her to complete all of her homework?

A. 45 minutes   B. 60 minutes   C. 90 minutes   D. 135 minutes

16. Are $4(x - 2) + 3(x - 1)$ and $7x + 2$ equivalent expressions? Justify your answer.

17. Roberta's dad has 20% of his salary withheld for taxes. If his salary is $78,000, how much is withheld for taxes?

A. $15,600   B. $20,000   C. $39,000   D. $50,000

18. Steve is making oatmeal. Typically, he uses $\frac{4}{3}$ cups of oatmeal and 3 cups of water. Today, he is making breakfast for his whole family, so he uses 12 cups of water. If he wants to keep the consistency of the oatmeal the same, how many cups of oatmeal should he use?

A. 4   B. $4\frac{2}{3}$ C. 5   D. $5\frac{1}{3}$

19. Miguel is making origami. He needs to start with a rectangular piece of paper that is $\frac{2}{3}$ feet long. If the total area of the piece of paper is $\frac{1}{9}$ square foot, how wide is the piece of paper?

   A. $\frac{1}{6}$ ft   B. $\frac{2}{27}$ ft   C. $\frac{5}{9}$ ft   D. $\frac{7}{9}$ ft

Use the story to answer questions 20 and 21.

A clerk puts a wooden crate on a scale and weighs it at 2 pounds. She begins filling the crate by emptying bags of dirt into it. After each bag, she weighs the crate and its contents again. With each bag she empties, the total weight increases by 8 pounds.

20. What is the independent variable? What is the dependent variable?

21. If *b* represents the number of bags of dirt and *w* represents the total weight of the crate and its contents, which equation shows the relationship between *b* and *w*?
    A. $b = 8w + 2$ B. $w = 8b + 2$ C. $b = 2w + 8$ D. $w = 2b + 8$

22. Which expression is equivalent to $\frac{1}{4}x - \frac{1}{2}(6x + 4) - 2\left(\frac{1}{8}x + 1\right)$?

   A. $-3x - 5$ B. $-3x - 4$ C. $-3x + 5$ D. $3x - 4$

23. Monique is selling magazines to help her school raise money. The school gets 35%, or 0.35, of every subscription Monique sells. Monique raised $56 for her school. Write and solve an equation to find the total subscription prices, *p*, of the magazines that Monique sold.

24. Which is the solution for the equation $x - 16 = 28$?
    A. *–12*   B. *12*   C. *16*   D. *44*

25. On a field trip, students have the option to have a turkey sub or a grilled cheese sandwich for lunch. If the school prepares 26 lunches and the ratio of subs to sandwiches is 8 to 5, how many students chose to have a grilled cheese sandwich for lunch?

 Answer Key

Question	Answer	Explanation	Standard
1	C	To divide a fraction by another fraction, multiply the first fraction by the reciprocal of the second fraction:	6.NS.A.1

$$\frac{2}{3} \div \frac{3}{8}$$
$$= \frac{2}{3} \times \frac{8}{3}$$
$$= \frac{2 \times 8}{3 \times 3}$$
$$= \frac{16}{9} = 1\frac{7}{9}$$

| 2 | 30 | This double number line diagram shows how to arrive at the answer. | 6.RP.A.3c |

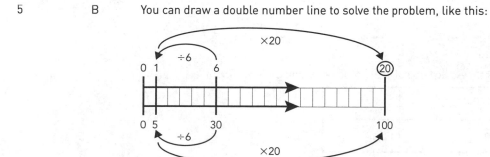

Scale 40% down to 10% percent by dividing by 4; divide 12 by 4 as well to get 3. Then scale 10% up to 100% by multiplying by 10; multiply 3 by 10 as well to get 30 CDs.

| 3 | C | This is a part-to-part ratio that compares dogs (5) to cats (2), so the correct ratio is 5:2. | 6.RP.A.2 |

| 4 | B | This double number line shows how to arrive at the solution: | 6.RP.A.3b |

| 5 | B | You can draw a double number line to solve the problem, like this: | 6.RP.A.3c |

Question	Answer	Explanation	Standard
6	C	The point on the right is 2 units to the right of and 7 units above the origin, so its coordinates are (2, 7). The point on the left is 6 units to the left of and 7 units above the origin, so its coordinates are (–6, 7).	6.NS.C.8
7	C	The points have the same y-coordinate, so the distance between them is the absolute value of the difference in their x-coordinates: $$\left|2-(-6)\right|=\left|2+6\right|=\left|8\right|=8$$ or $$\left|-6-2\right|=\left|-8\right|=8$$	6.NS.C.8
8	D	Write a mathematical sentence in words: the price of the book, $15, plus the tax is equal to the total cost, $16.05. Then translate the sentence using numbers, letters, and symbols: $15 + t = 16.05$, which is the same as $t + 15 = 16.05$.	6.EE.B.7
9	C	Solve the equation by substituting each of the possible solutions into the equation to see which one makes it true. $$3x+14=-1$$ $$3(-16)+14=-1 \qquad 3(-12)+14=-1$$ $$-48+14=-1 \qquad -36+14=-1$$ $$-34\neq-1 \qquad -22\neq-1$$ $$3(-5)+14=-1 \qquad 3(5)+14=-1$$ $$-15+14=-1 \qquad 15+14=-1$$ $$-1=-1 \qquad 29\neq-1$$ The solution is $x = -5$ because it is the only value that makes the equation true.	6.EE.B.5
10	120 mins	This table shows how to solve the problem using repeated addition. 	Miles	1	2	3	4	5	6	 	Minutes	20	40	60	80	100	120		6.RP.A.3 , 6.RP.A.3a
11	A	Let t represent the amount of money that Tina has. Jim has 3 times as much, or $3t$, and the total amount they have together is $12, so solve the equation $t + 3t = 12$. $$t + 3t = 12 \longrightarrow 4t = 12 \longrightarrow \frac{4t}{4} = \frac{12}{4} \longrightarrow t = 3$$	6.EE.B.7
12	C	This table shows how to solve the problem using multiplication:	6.RP.A.3d

For question 10:

Miles	1	2	3	4	5	6
Minutes	20	40	60	80	100	120

For question 12:

Kilograms	1	35 (1 × 35)
Pounds	2.2	77 (2.2 × 35)

Question	Answer	Explanation	Standard
13	C	To write the equation, look for a pattern in the table. Start with a word equation: the number of teaspoons of salt equals 3 times the number of servings of chili, so the equation is $t = 3c$. You can check the answer by substituting each pair of values from the table into the equation: $3 = 3(1)$, $6 = 3(2)$, $9 = 3(3)$, $12 = 3(4)$.	6.EE.C.9
14	B	Look at the graph. Find 1 cup of cranberry juice on the vertical axis and read the corresponding number of cups of grape juice on the horizontal axis. For every 1 cup of cranberry juice, there are 2 cups of grape juice, so the ratio of cranberry juice to grape juice is 1:2.	6.RP.A.3a
15	D	This table shows how to solve the problem using multiplication:	6.RP.A.3b

Courses	2	6 (2×3)
Minutes	45	135 (45×3)

Question	Answer	Explanation	Standard
16	No	$4(x - 2) + 3(x - 1)$ $= 4x - 8 + 3x - 3$ $= 7x - 11$ $7x - 11 \neq 7x + 2$	6.EE.A.4
17	A	To scale 100% down to 20%, divide by 5. This means that to scale \$78,000 to 20% of \$78,000, divide by 5 as well: \$78,000 ÷ 5 = \$15,600.	6.RP.A.3c
18	D	This table shows how to solve the problem using multiplication:	6.RP.A.3

Water (cups)	3	12 (3×4)
Oatmeal (cups)	$\frac{4}{3}$	$5\frac{1}{3}$ $(\frac{4}{3} \times 4)$

Question	Answer	Explanation	Standard
19	A	You can find the area of a rectangle by multiplying the length times the width, $A = l \times w$. If you know the area, you can find one of the dimensions by dividing the area by the other dimension. Here, you know the area and the length, so divide to find the width: $$\frac{1}{9} \div \frac{2}{3} = \frac{1}{9} \times \frac{3}{2} = \frac{1 \times 3}{9 \times 2} = \frac{3}{18} = \frac{1}{6}.$$	6.NS.A.1
20	Dependent: total weight Independent: number of bags of dirt	The dependent variable is weight because it depends on the number of bags of dirt. The independent variable is the number of bags of dirt	6.EE.C.9
21	B	As the clerk adds each bag, the total weight increases by 8 pounds, so the unit rate is 8. The starting amount is the weight of the empty crate, which is 2 pounds, so the equation is $w = 8b + 2$.	6.EE.C.9

Question	Answer	Explanation	Standard
22	B	Apply the distributive property, then apply the commutative property of addition, and finally, combine like terms to simplify the expression:	6.EE.A.3

$$\frac{1}{4}x - \frac{1}{2}(6x+4) - 2\left(\frac{1}{8}x+1\right)$$

$$= \frac{1}{4}x - \frac{1}{2}(6x) - \frac{1}{2}(4) - 2\left(\frac{1}{8}x\right) - 2(1)$$

$$= \frac{1}{4}x - 3x - 2 - \frac{1}{4}x - 2$$

$$= \frac{1}{4}x - 3x - \frac{1}{4}x - 2 - 2$$

$$= -3x - 4$$

Question	Answer	Explanation	Standard
23	$160	Write the equation in words, then translate it to numbers and symbols: 0.35 times the total amount of the subscription costs is equal to the contribution to school. The equation is $0.35p = 56$. Then use inverse operations to solve for p. The inverse of multiplication is division, so divide both sides of the equation by 0.35 to find that the total amount Monique sold was $160.	6.EE.B.7
24	D	Use inverse operations to isolate x.	6.EE.B.7

$$x - 16 = 28$$
$$x - 16 + 16 = 28 + 16$$
$$x = 44$$

Question	Answer	Explanation	Standard
25	10	You can solve the problem by drawing a tape diagram, like this:	6.RP.A.3

Turkey Subs | 2 | 2 | 2 | 2 | 2 | 2 | 2 | 2 |

Grilled Cheese Sandwiches | 2 | 2 | 2 | 2 | 2 |

There are 13 parts in all, so each part represents 2 students, which means that $5 \times 2 = 10$ students chose a grilled cheese sandwich.

OVERVIEW

For Grade 6, the ELA Common Core Standards build upon skills learned in previous grades. For informational passages, the standards require students to evaluate bias in texts, and to determine the validity of evidence and arguments that are presented. For literary passages, students are expected to be able to explain plot sequences and how characters change as the plot advances. For writing, students are expected to write opinion pieces that utilize relevant evidence, and to use planning and revising to help create stronger writing.

Listed below are the ELA Common Core Standards for Grade 6 that we have identified as "power standards." We consider these standards to be critical for your child's success. Each lesson in this section focuses on a single power standard so that you and your child may practice that standard to achieve mastery. The applicable standards are divided into three categories: Reading—Informational Text; Reading—Literature; and Writing.

Reading—Informational Text

CCSS.ELA-Literacy.RI.6.1: Cite textual evidence to support analysis of what the text says explicitly as well as inferences drawn from the text.

CCSS.ELA-Literacy.RI.6.2: Determine a central idea of a text and how it is conveyed through particular details; provide a summary of the text distinct from personal opinions or judgments.

CCSS.ELA-Literacy.RI.6.4: Determine the meaning of words and phrases as they are used in a text, including figurative, connotative, and technical meanings.

CCSS.ELA-Literacy.RI.6.8: Trace and evaluate the argument and specific claims in a text, distinguishing claims that are supported by reasons and evidence from claims that are not.

Reading—Literature

CCSS.ELA-Literacy.RL.6.1: Cite textual evidence to support analysis of what the text says explicitly as well as inferences drawn from the text.

CCSS.ELA-Literacy.RL.6.2: Determine a theme or central idea of a text and how it is conveyed through particular details; provide a summary of the text distinct from personal opinions or judgments.

CCSS.ELA-Literacy.RL.6.3: Describe how a particular story's or drama's plot unfolds in a series of episodes as well as how the characters respond or change as the plot moves toward a resolution.

CCSS.ELA-Literacy.RL.6.4: Determine the meaning of words and phrases as they are used in a text, including figurative and connotative meanings; analyze the impact of a specific word choice on meaning and tone.

Writing

CCSS.ELA-Literacy.W.6.1: Write arguments to support claims with clear reasons and relevant evidence.

CCSS.ELA-Literacy.W.6.5: With some guidance and support from peers and adults, develop and strengthen writing as needed by planning, revising, editing, rewriting, or trying a new approach.

READING

For the reading standards, Common Core breaks texts into two basic types: (1) Informational Texts, which essentially cover all types of nonfiction; and (2) Literature, which includes stories, drama, and poetry. The following chart from the Common Core Standards Initiative Web site provides a brief overview of the range of text types. For the purposes of assessment, texts are also selected from a broad range of cultures and time periods.

Literature			Informational Text
Stories	Dramas	Poetry	Literary Nonfiction and Historical, Scientific, and Technical Texts
Includes children's adventure stories, folktales, legends, fables, fantasy, realistic fiction, and myth	Includes staged dialogue and brief familiar scenes	Includes nursery rhymes and the subgenres of the narrative poem, limerick, and free verse poem	Includes biographies and autobiographies; books about history, social studies, science, and the arts; technical texts, including directions, forms, and information displayed in graphs, charts, or maps; and digital sources on a range of topics

As practice is the best way to build reading skills, encourage your child to read a variety of literary works and informational texts.

Informational Text

Informational texts include literary nonfiction, such as biographies or memoirs, as well as historical, scientific, and technical texts. They include expository, persuasive, and functional texts in the form of personal essays, opinion pieces, speeches, essays, journalism, and other nonfiction accounts. A variety of types of informational texts is included in this section to give your child practice across a range of genres and subgenres.

Literature

The literature category includes three main subcategories: stories, dramas, and poetry. Stories may be adventure stories, realistic fiction, folktales and fables, legends and myths, and fantasy. Dramas include the written text that would be used for a play, with dialogue, stage directions, and scenes. Poetry includes nursery rhymes, narrative poems, limericks, and free verse. A variety of stories is included in this section of the book to give your child practice with the genre used most commonly on tests. Because practice is the best way to build reading skills, encourage your child to read a variety of literary works.

WRITING

The Common Core Standards for writing are tied closely to reading. Many of the skills your child learns to read effectively are also applicable to their own writing. In general, your child will be asked to write short passages that express a specific viewpoint or support a specific argument. For these writing passages, the emphasis will be on using information, details, and examples to support the main idea or ideas. Your child will also be expected to create writing that flows smoothly, with an introductory sentence or paragraph, a main body, and a closing sentence or paragraph. In addition to writing an effective draft, your child will also be asked to revise, adjust, and improve their own writing and the writing of others.

Another critical element is mastery of basic grammar and mechanics appropriate for his or her grade level. This is shown through your child's own writing, as well as through revising and improving the writing of others.

THE STANDARD

RI.6.1: *Supporting Evidence and Inferences – Informational Text*
Cite textual evidence to support analysis of what the text says explicitly as well as inferences drawn from the text.

What does it mean?

This informational standard focuses on a student's ability to comprehend the information that is stated in a passage as well as draw inferences based on information in the passage.

Try this together

Let's use the following text as an example of the kind of informational passage your child might encounter in school. To address this reading standard, a teacher might ask questions such as the ones that follow the passage, or assign them as homework. We have provided possible answers in the "Answers" section, along with an explanation of how the questions connect to the standard.

Before trying this exercise with your child, read through the passage and the questions that follow it. Then have your child read the passage aloud to you and answer the questions. Talk about the answers together. Help your child realize that he or she can find answers to questions by looking back at the passage for clues.

The Silk Road

During the first century, silk and other goods were highly desirable items in ancient Rome. Caravans carried these goods from China to Rome. The route used by traders was known as the Silk Road. This name—which actually refers to several different routes—was first used by a German scholar, von Richthofen.

The merchants had a choice of routes. Some merchants followed the road leading to the Caspian Sea by passing through the Afghan valleys, while some preferred to climb the Karakorum Mountains. They arrived in Asia Minor by way of Iran. They traveled enormous distances. The routes went through rugged and harsh land, including deserts and mountains. Finally they would arrive in what is Italy today.

The Silk Road was extremely important at the time. The Silk Road had a powerful impact on the goods that were available. Caravans heading toward China carried gold, ivory, and glass. In the opposite direction, furs, ceramics, jade, lacquer, and iron as well as silk were carried to Rome.

But the Silk Road was also important because it was a way to exchange ideas. Rome and China were the greatest civilizations of the period. They had much to offer one another.

These routes were the established ways of travel even when Marco Polo took the Silk Road to reach China.

The Silk Road declined after safer ships allowed traders to sail between the Roman Empire and China directly. But these water routes were not without their difficulties either. Weather and pirates were always a threat.

Today the Silk Road is making a comeback as a tourist attraction. The remains of old cities and grottoes are a boon to archaeologists too. The route is significant because it offers an insight into civilizations of a different time.

Questions

1. Why was the Silk Road important?

_____

_____

2. Besides goods, what else did the Silk Road provide?

_____

_____

3. Which sentence supports the inference that travel over land between China and Rome was not easy?

_____

_____

4. Why did traders begin using the Silk Road less and less?

_____

_____

5. Why is the Silk Road popular today?

_____

_____

Answers

1. Why was the Silk Road important? *The Silk Road was important because it allowed traders to exchange goods from far away. This question requires students to interpret the explicit information to form a conclusion, a higher task than simply locating explicit information.*
2. Besides goods, what else did the Silk Road provide? *The Silk Road also provided an*

exchange of ideas. This question requires students to review the passage and find explicit information.

3. Which sentence supports the inference that travel over land between China and Rome was not easy? *"The routes went through rugged and harsh land, including deserts and mountains." This question requires students to find supporting evidence for an inference.*

4. Why did traders begin using the Silk Road less and less? *Safer ships made the Silk Road less desirable. This question requires students to interpret explicit information.*

5. Why is the Silk Road popular today? *Tourists are interested in visiting the Silk Road. This question requires students to find explicit information in the passage.*

Extra practice

To help your child work on the skills assessed by this standard, try this activity:

1. First ask your child to reread the "The Silk Road."
2. Then ask him or her to make a list of items that were sent to China and a list of items that were sent to Rome.

Have your child infer why these items were traded.

Then discuss this inference and what information supports it.

Through this activity your child will be directly practicing the skills listed in the standard. He or she will identify explicit information and then form an inference based on it. The discussion of why these items were traded will most likely touch upon the fact that Rome and China did not have the items that were traded back and forth.. Praise your child for this work, explaining exactly what skills were used in this activity.

Quiz

Have your child read this passage and write the answers independently in the space provided.

 ## Marian Anderson

Marian Anderson was an African American woman and a great singer. She was also a remarkable person. Her voice was admired by people all over the world. She was also the first black person to sing at the Metropolitan Opera House in New York City, a premier hall for great singers. It took Anderson a long time to sing there. She had to overcome prejudice, but she refused to give up. She was almost 58 when she sang at the Met.

Marian Anderson was born in 1897 and lived in Philadelphia, Pennsylvania. She began singing in her church choir when she was only five. Later, she sang solos at other churches. Everyone agreed that she had a wonderful voice, and they encouraged her. By the time she was fifteen, Anderson knew she wanted to be a professional singer, but she had no real training until she was seventeen. Her family could not afford to pay for lessons, so her teacher gave her lessons free of charge. Other teachers taught her without pay, too.

Marian Anderson went to study voice in Europe. People loved her voice there. She sang in many concert halls, in many countries. When the great musician Arturo Toscanini heard Anderson sing, he was amazed. He is reported to have said, "A voice like yours is heard only once in a hundred years."

She toured Japan, Israel, and India and won many awards. She was famous around the world. Eventually, Americans became interested in her and she returned to the United States to tour this country. In 1955, she appeared at the Metropolitan Opera House. Just before she retired, she sang at President John F. Kennedy's inauguration. That was a great day for her.

Even as a child, Marian Anderson faced prejudice. She wanted to go to a music high school in Philadelphia, but she could not because she was black. On her many tours of America, she faced racial prejudice. Some hotels would not let her stay there and some restaurants would not let her eat there. But many people loved her. She was told she could not sing in Constitution Hall in Washington, D.C., so she was invited to sing at the Lincoln Memorial instead and some 75,000 people came to hear her sing.

Marian Anderson said she was "an artist not a fighter" and is remembered for her wonderful contralto voice. But she was a fighter in her own way. She helped stop prejudice. She helped change the course for future generations of African Americans.

Questions

1. Read the sentence from the story: "She was told she could not sing in Constitution Hall in Washington, D.C., so she was invited to sing at the Lincoln Memorial instead and some 75,000 people came to hear her sing." What inference does the sentence support?

   _____

   _____

2. What is suggested by Marian Anderson saying she was "an artist not a fighter"?

   _____

   _____

3. Where did Marian Anderson first become famous?

   _____

   _____

4. Why was singing at the Metropolitan Opera House important to Marian Anderson?

   _____

   _____

5. How did Marian Anderson help stop prejudice?

 **Answers**

Questions 1 and 2 require the student to interpret the explicit information in the text to make an inference. Question 3 requires students to look back and locate explicit information. Questions 4 and 5 requires students to analyze the explicit information in the passage.

1. Read the sentence from the story: She was told she could not sing in Constitution Hall in Washington, D.C., so she was invited to sing at the Lincoln Memorial and some 75,000 people came to hear her sing. What inference does the sentence support? *People wanted to show support for Marian Anderson.*

2. What is suggested by Marian Anderson saying she was "an artist not a fighter"? *It suggests that she felt strongly about her singing and, while she did stand up for herself, that was not the most important thing to her.*

3. Where did Marian Anderson first become famous? *In Europe*

4. Why was singing at the Metropolitan Opera House important to Marian Anderson? *It showed that she was one of the greatest singers, since only the greatest singers performed there.*

5. How did Marian Anderson help stop prejudice? *She continued to sing and face the prejudice she encountered without ever giving up.*

THE STANDARD

RI.6.2: *Central Idea and Key Details – Informational Text*
Determine a central idea of a text and how it is conveyed through particular details; provide a summary of the text distinct from personal opinions or judgments.

What does it mean?

This informational standard focuses on a student's ability to analyze the central or main idea of a passage and how the details support it; it also focuses on a student's ability to summarize the passage without including personal opinions or judgments.

Try this together

Let's use the following text as an example of the kind of informational passage your child might encounter in school. To address this reading standard, a teacher might ask questions such as the ones that follow the passage, or assign them as homework. We have provided possible answers in the "Answers" section, along with an explanation of how the questions connect to the standard.

Before trying this exercise with your child, read through the passage and the questions that follow it. Then have your child read the passage aloud to you and answer the questions. Talk about the answers together. Help your child realize that she can find answers to questions by looking back at the passage for clues.

 Olana

One of the most beautiful houses in the world was built by an artist named Frederic Church. Church traveled extensively and was influenced by the various cultures he encountered while traveling. In particular, he was struck by Persian and Moorish architecture found mainly in North Africa and the Middle East. These designs often included arched windows, balconies, and towers made of stone, as well as colorful decorative tiles.

This style of building was exciting to Frederic Church. It seemed mysterious to him and was very different from the buildings that he had seen in America. He wanted to build a home in such a style for himself and his family.

Before he built the house, Church spent a very long time making sketches of it. He worked with an architect, but he did most of the design. In order to see what the house would look like, he drew pictures of everything. He drew the designs that would be on the building and pictures of where the furniture would go. He also decided where in the house he would hang the many wonderful paintings he had done.

Church had many acres of land along a beautiful river in New York. He tried to figure out the best spot for his new home. There was one area that was on a hill overlooking the river. He chose this spot because from the house, he could see the river and nearby mountains.

After the house was built, Church planted flowers, bushes, and trees in places where they would look beautiful. Then he made paintings of the land and the house that he loved so much. Church named it Olana, after a treasure castle in Persia. The house was his treasure because it was where he and his wife and children lived. The house was very different from any other house in America.

Today, many people visit Olana. They come to see this magnificent building where time seems to stand still. They love to see the house because it looks today just the way it looked when Church lived there many years ago. Visitors to the house can see the same furniture that the Churches used. They can learn what toys the Church children played with and what foods the family served their guests. Thousands of people come each year to see Olana.

Frederic Church was a man with a vision. He was inspired to create his dream home, and he did just that. Today, people can still enjoy the results of his creativity.

? Questions

1. What detail best supports the idea that Frederic Church wanted to do most of the designing of his house?

   _____

   _____

2. Why does the author of the passage include the detail that thousands of people come to see Olana each year?

   _____

   _____

3. Why did Frederic Church choose Persian and Moorish styles for his house?

   _____

   _____

4. What is one detail that would not be included in a summary of the passage?

   _____

   _____

5. Based on information in the passage, what inference can you make about Frederic Church?

   _____

   _____

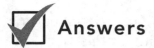 **Answers**

1. What detail best supports the idea that Frederic Church wanted to do most of the designing of his house? *Church drew pictures of all parts of the house and drew the designs that would go on the building. This question requires students to find details that support the central idea.*

2. Why does the author of the passage include the detail that thousands of people come to see Olana each year? *This detail shows that Olana is a popular place for tourists today. This question requires students to make an inference based on the details in the passage. This requires students to analyze an author's reasons for including information.*

3. Why did Frederic Church choose the Moorish style for his house? *Church thought the Moorish style was mysterious and different. This question requires students to look for relevant details that explain this central idea.*

4. What is one detail that would not be included in a summary of the passage? *Answers will vary, but accept any details that seem minor in nature, such as the fact that Moorish/Persian architecture has arched windows, or that Church had many acres of land. This question requires students to analyze the various details and decide which are important enough to include in a summary and which are not. This develops the students' analytical skills.*

5. Based on information in the passage, what inference can you make about Frederic Church? *Answers will vary; accept inferences that are supported by details in the passage. Possible answer: He was very creative and also appreciated beautiful objects and surroundings. This question requires students to combine various details so that a conclusion can be made about the subject.*

Extra practice

To help your child work on the skills assessed by this standard, try this activity:

1. First ask your child to reread the passage "Olana."
2. Then ask your child to choose three paragraphs in the passage and state the central idea of each one.
3. Ask your child to write down two details that support each central idea.
4. Discuss the differences between central ideas and supporting details.

Through this activity, your child will be directly practicing the skills covered by the standard. He or she will *determine the central ideas of different paragraphs* through the details and will discuss with you what the difference is between a central idea and a supporting detail. This is central to understanding this standard. Praise your child for this work, explaining exactly what skills were used during the activity.

Have your child read this passage and write the answers independently in the space provided.

 ## Army Ants

Army ants are predators. An insect that is attacked by army ants stands no chance. The army ants of Africa and South America live in groups of 10,000 to 500,000. They travel together looking for food. They attack animals in their path. Together, they are so powerful that they can kill tarantulas, lizards, birds, snakes, or pigs.

There are about 150 different kinds of army ants traveling around Central and South America and the southern United States. A single colony of army ants may contain as many as one million ants. A colony can eat 50,000 insects in one day. Because of that, army ants run out of food quickly and must keep moving to find new food.

Army ants live for the most part in the tropical regions of India, Africa, and South America. Sometimes they are found as far north as the Mississippi Valley and as far south as Patagonia, a part of the South American country of Argentina.

The ants in the Mississippi Valley and Patagonia are very different. They are usually more than one inch long. The males look different from the females and are also different from the workers. For that reason, scientists have sometimes thought that the males are a different kind of ant. The queens are wingless, while the males are winged. The males look more like a wasp. The workers vary in appearance. Some are very large with powerful jaws, while others are smaller.

One of the great wonders is to see is a colony of army ants on the march. They look amazingly like columns of humans marching. There are groups of small workers and large-jawed workers on either side of the main columns of ants that act as scouts. They move ahead, laying scent trails to mark the way for the main body of marchers. In many cases, the main body is so large that it breaks up into several smaller groups. Sometimes the main body of ants will move underground, building tunnels and moving quickly and quietly so that their presence is a secret.

Although the army ants feed mainly on insects, little to nothing escapes their attack. Although many of the stories about the attacks of army ants have been exaggerated, there are records of tied-up horses being found with nothing but a skeleton left after being attacked.

Even though they are dangerous, army ants can be helpful by ridding an area of unwanted creatures. In parts of South America, army ants are welcome because they kill vermin, rats, mice, spiders, cockroaches, and other pests. This means residents do not have to use dangerous insecticides. Villagers often leave their homes when army ants are coming. When they return, they have completely insect-free houses.

Questions

1. What detail is not important to a summary of the story?

   _____

   _____

2. What are three important details that should be included in a summary?

_____

_____

3. Which sentence in paragraph 4 states the paragraph's central idea?

_____

_____

4. Read the sentence from the passage: "Army ants are predators." What are two details that support this central idea in paragraph 1?

_____

_____

_____

5. Why do the villagers of South America like army ants? Use details from the story to support your answer.

_____

_____

_____

_____

 **Answers**

Questions 1 and 2 require the student to evaluate the details in a passage and decide which details are important and which are not important enough to include in a summary. Question 3 requires that students to figure out a central idea from the details in a paragraph while questions 4 and 5 asks students to identify details that support a central idea.

1. What detail is not important to a summary of the story? *Answers will vary, but accept any details that seem minor in nature, such as the fact that Patagonia is a part of the South American country of Argentina.*

2. What are three important details that should be included in a summary? *Possible answers include: Army ants are predators. Army ants travel in large groups eating everything and killing animals. Army ants kill unwanted animals for South American villagers.*

3. Which sentence from paragraph 4 states the paragraph's central idea? *The ants in the Mississippi Valley and Patagonia are very different.*

4. Read the sentence from the passage: "Army ants are predators." Which two details support this central idea in paragraph 1? *They attack animals in their path. Together*

13

they are so powerful that they can kill tarantulas, lizards, birds, snakes, or pigs.

5. Why do the villagers of South America like army ants? Use details from the passage to support your answer. *The army ants kill unwanted animals, like insects and vermin. The villagers leave their homes when the army ants come and when they return their homes are free of insects.*

THE STANDARD

RI.6.8: *Analyzing an Argument – Informational Text*
Trace and evaluate the argument and specific claims in a text, distinguishing claims that are supported by reasons and evidence from claims that are not.

What does it mean?

This informational standard focuses on a student's ability to evaluate an argument and claims in a passage and being able to tell which claims are supported by evidence and which claims are not supported.

Try this together

Let's use the following text as an example of the kind of persuasive passage your child might encounter in school. To address this reading standard, a teacher might ask questions such as the ones that follow the passage, or assign them as homework. We have provided possible answers in the "Answers" section, along with an explanation of how the questions connect to the standard.

Before trying this exercise with your child, read through the passage and the questions that follow it. Then have your child read the passage aloud to you and answer the questions. Talk about the answers together. Help your child realize that he or she can find answers to questions by looking back at the passage for clues.

The Amazon Rain Forest

The Amazon rain forest is one of the largest rain forests in the world. It covers nearly half of the South American continent and includes parts of Brazil, Ecuador, Bolivia, Peru, and Colombia.

The trees in this vast forest are very valuable for furniture, paper, and lumber, so they attract the interest of large logging companies from many parts of the world. The companies are required to plant new trees to replace the trees cut down, but some greedy companies do not comply with the law. These companies fail to replace the trees they destroy. In addition, some people burn down areas of forest to make room for farms and new homes. For these reasons and others, the rain forest is being destroyed.

This destruction is a tragedy. There are certain rare birds and animals that live only in the rain forest. They will be lost forever. Many people also live there, so the loss of the rain forest means the loss of their homes and way of life as well.

All over the world, temperatures are rising, and this is dangerous to many forms of life. This global warming comes about because of increased carbon dioxide from vehicles that burn fossil fuels. The rain forest naturally helps keep carbon dioxide levels low, so the rain forest helps diminish the effects of global warming. If we don't preserve the rain forest, the earth will get too hot.

While all of the reasons to preserve the rain forest are notable, this one seems to be the most significant, and I believe it will have the most far-reaching impact.

For all of these reasons, I think it is important to take action to save the Amazon rain forest. Some people are suggesting that we boycott everything that comes from the forest. That's mainly wood like mahogany, which is used to make furniture. I think this is a very good idea. Companies won't cut down mahogany trees if they can't sell the wood. I support the boycott and I encourage you to support it as well.

Questions

1. What is the author's main argument?

   _____

   _____

2. Read the sentence that follows: "If we don't preserve the rain forest, the earth will get too hot." Which sentence supports this claim?

   _____

   _____

3. Read the sentence that follows: "The companies are required to plant new trees to replace the trees cut down, but some greedy companies do not comply with the law." Which claim made in this sentence is not supported in the passage?

   _____

   _____

4. Read the sentence that follows: "This destruction is a tragedy." Which sentence or sentences support this claim?

   _____

   _____

5. What reasons does the author give as evidence that the rain forest is being destroyed?

   _____

   _____

Answers

1. What is the author's main argument? *The author's main argument is that the Amazon rain forest should be protected. This question requires students to analyze the entire passage and figure out the main argument.*

2. Read the sentence that follows: "If we don't preserve the rain forest, the earth will get too hot." Which sentence supports this claim? *"The rain forest naturally helps keep carbon dioxide levels low, so the rain forest helps diminish the effects of global warming." This question requires students to look for evidence that the claim is supported.*

3. Read the sentence that follows: "The companies are required to plant new trees to replace the trees cut down, but some greedy companies do not comply with the law." Which claim made in this sentence is not supported in the passage? *The unsupported claim is that some companies are greedy. No evidence is given to support this opinion. This question requires students to analyze what claim is made in the sentence and whether there is any evidence that supports it.*

4. Read the sentence that follows: "This destruction is a tragedy." Which sentence or sentences support this claim? *"There are certain rare birds and animals that live only in the rain forest. They will be lost forever. Many people live also there, so the loss of the rain forest means the loss of their homes and way of life as well." This question requires students to look for evidence that supports this claim.*

5. What reasons does the author give as evidence that the rain forest is being destroyed? *Trees are being cut down for wood, paper, and other items; companies are not replanting the trees; people are destroying rain forests to use the land for farming. This question requires students to look through the passage and find any evidence as to how the Amazon rain forests are being destroyed.*

Extra practice

To help your child work on the skills assessed by this standard, try this activity:

1. First ask your child to reread the passage.
2. Then ask your child to make a chart listing the claims made in the passage in one column.
3. In the next column, have your child list any evidence that supports the claims.
4. Then discuss the claims and supporting evidence or lack of it.

Through this activity your child will be directly practicing the skills covered by the standard. He or she will identify arguments and claims as well as supporting evidence. He or she will learn to distinguish between claims that are supported and those that are not. This is central to understanding this standard that requires identification arguments and claims and supporting evidence as well as knowing which claims are supported and which are not.

Praise your child for this work, explaining exactly what skills were used in this activity.

? Quiz

Persuasive passages about current issues are commonly read in the sixth grade. Have your child read this passage and write the answers independently in the space provided.

 **Working Teens**

We seem to think we have solved all the problems of child labor, but that simply isn't the case. All over the country there are teens who are working long hours and not being properly paid for it. And while teens think they have good reasons for working, work may actually interfere with their education and health.

The number of American teens with jobs today is larger than ever before. Some teens work almost full-time. But they get paid for part-time hours. Often teenagers, and their parents, either don't care or don't know the rules regarding how late in the evening they can work. The consequences are that teens may not be spending enough time on homework, or may not be getting enough sleep.

According to current regulations, fourteen- and fifteen-year-old teens are only supposed to work as long as the job does not interfere with school. Other rules say that this age group is not allowed to operate heavy or dangerous machinery or to work after 10 p.m. But I fear that happens more often than we know. Teenagers between sixteen and seventeen may work until 12 midnight, but they must have a Parent Consent Form to do so.

I believe that problems arise when the rules for teenagers working are not enforced. These rules are necessary. They must be obeyed by both the teenager and the employer. I think that parents should be more watchful of their teenage children and make sure that they are not working too many hours, or too late at night.

Today, young adults have many reasons for working. Some want to pay for a car or automobile insurance, and some are trying to save up money for college. A few may be trying to help their parents out. More likely, many just want to be able to buy clothes, music, or video games.

Kids are happy to get a job and make a good amount of money. And parents usually are happy to see them occupied in a way that they think is productive.

But the truth is that many teens spend too much time at work, and do not have time to study for tests and other projects. This means their grades go down. Some parents seem unaware of the connection between the long hours on the job and poor grades. Another problem with working is that when teens finally do have a little free time, they need to relax. They don't want to study.

I believe it is time for schools to hold informational meetings with teens and their parents to explain the consequences of working too much. Do these kids really need to have a car, a new wardrobe, or a new sound system? Is it worth losing out on doing the best they can in school, or playing sports, or being in the choir or band, or having a social life? I think that parents and schools should reexamine what is most important, and advise teens against taking a job that will require too many hours of work.

 Questions

1. What is the main argument of the passage?

   _____

   _____

2. Read the sentence that follows: "Today, young adults have many reasons for working." Which sentence or sentences support this claim?

   _____

   _____

3. Read the sentence that follows: "The number of teens with jobs today is larger than ever before in the U.S." What additional information would make this claim stronger?

   _____

   _____

4. Read the sentence that follows: "And parents usually are happy to see them occupied in a way that they think is productive." What is this claim based on?

   _____

   _____

5. How does the author conclude the argument?

   _____

   _____

✓ Answers

Questions 1 and 5 require the student to analyze the overall argument of the passage. Question 2 requires students to find evidence to support the claim. Question 3 requires students to figure out what kind of information could be added to the passage to make this claim more valid. Question 4 requires students to analyze the type of claim that is being made.

1. What is the main argument of the passage? *The main argument is that students are working so much that they are hurting their ability to become educated.*

2. Read the sentence that follows: "Today, young adults have many reasons for working." Which sentence or sentences support this claim? *"Some want to pay for a car or automobile insurance, and some are trying to save up money for college. A few may be trying to help their parents out. More likely, just want to be able to buy clothes, CDs, or computer games."*

3. Read the sentence that follows: "The number of teens with jobs today is larger than

ever before in the U.S." What additional information would make this claim stronger? *Answers may vary. Possible answer: Statistics from a trusted source about how many teens are working today as compared with other years*

4. Read the sentence that follows: "And parents usually are happy to see them occupied in a way that they think is productive." What is this claim based on? *This claim is based on personal opinion.*

5. How does the author conclude the argument? *The author concludes the argument by suggesting that schools hold informational meetings for teens and parents to explain the problems associated with working too much, such as neglecting school work.*

THE STANDARD

RI.6.4: *Vocabulary – Informational Text*
Determine the meaning of words and phrases as they are used in a text, including figurative, connotative, and technical meanings.

What does it mean?

This informational standard focuses on a student's ability to comprehend words and phrases in a text, including words and phrases that are used figuratively as well as to understand the connotation (or associated meaning) of words or phrases through the use of context clues, whenever possible. It also requires that students comprehend technical meanings.

This standard is related to other general vocabulary standards that are part of the Vocabulary Acquisition and Use section of Common Core Language skills. The standard is sometimes tested in connection with those other standards, which are included here for easy reference:

L.6.4: Determine or clarify the meaning of unknown and multiple-meaning word and phrases based on grade 6 reading and content, choosing flexibly from a range of strategies.

- *L.6.4a:* Use context (e.g., the overall meaning of a sentence or paragraph; a word's position of function in a sentence) as a clue to the meaning of a word or phrase.
- *L.6.4b:* Use common, grade-appropriate Greek or Latin affixes and roots as clues to the meaning of a word (e.g., *audience, auditory, audible*).
- *L.6.4c:* Consult reference materials (e.g., dictionaries, glossaries, thesauruses), both print and digital, to find the pronunciation of a word or determine or clarify its precise meaning or its part of speech.
- *L.6.4d:* Verify the preliminary determination of the meaning of a word or phrase (e.g., by checking the inferred meaning in context or in a dictionary).

L.6.5: Demonstrate understanding of figurative language, word relationships, and nuances in word meanings.

- *L.6.5a:* Interpret figures of speech (e.g., personification) in context.
- *L.6.5b:* Use the relationship between particular words (e.g., cause/effect, part/whole, item/category) to better understand each of the words.
- *L.6.5c:* Distinguish among the connotations (associations) of words with similar denotations (definitions) (e.g., *stingy, scrimping, economical, unwasteful, thrifty*).

As you can see from the vocabulary-related standards, success in this area requires students to be able to decipher word meaning using the context in which it is used and knowledge of root words and affixes (prefixes and suffixes). Students also will need to recognize the figurative and connotative use of language. (Figurative language involves the use of words or phrases in a way that is not their literal, or dictionary, meaning.)

Try this together

Let's use the following text as an example of the kind of passage your child might encounter in school. To address this reading standard, a teacher might ask questions such as the ones that follow the passage, or assign them as homework. We have provided possible answers in the "Answers" section, along with an explanation of how the questions connect to the standard.

Before trying this exercise with your child, read through the passage and the questions that follow it. Then have your child read the passage aloud to you and answer the questions. Talk about the answers together. Help your child realize that he or she can find answers to questions by looking back at the passage for clues:

 **Vitamins**

Vitamins are a vital part of a person's diet; they are necessary to your health. Your body needs them to do its work. You don't need big amounts of vitamins, since small amounts are enough, but you must have them. Lack of vitamins can damage your eyes, your teeth, and your bones. If you do not have enough vitamins, many parts of your body will not function properly.

Most people get adequate vitamins from their food, so they do not need any vitamin pills. If you eat a variety of foods, you probably get enough vitamins and do not need supplements. The right kind of food is important. Milk, bread, and cereals all have vitamins. Vegetables, fruits, and meat also contain vitamins. If you eat some of each of these foods, you will probably get all the vitamins you need.

Some countries don't have enough food for everyone, so many people in these countries have poor diets; this means that they don't get enough vitamins. Even in countries where there is enough food for everyone, some people don't get the nutrients they require. Perhaps they eat just a few foods. For example, some people can't eat milk or anything that contains milk, and other people can't eat things made of wheat. A few people dislike vegetables and won't eat anything green. Also, people who want to lose weight may not always eat a balanced diet. All of these people run the risk of not getting enough vitamins from their food, so they may need to take vitamin pills.

Different vitamins keep different parts of your body in good shape. People who don't get enough vitamins may develop deficiency diseases. These diseases can be serious, but people usually get well as soon as their bodies get enough vitamins again.

Each vitamin is important. Vitamin A helps you see and it also keeps your skin healthy and fresh. Vitamin A is stored in our bodies, so most of us have enough. If you don't have enough Vitamin A, you may become blind and your skin may get rough and dry.

There are many kinds of Vitamin B. These B vitamins help you digest your food and help you produce red blood cells. Without Vitamin B, you can suffer from many problems. For instance, your muscles may ache, your skin may be prone to sores, or you may become dizzy. People without enough vitamin B12 may become anemic, which means they don't have enough red blood cells.

Other vitamins also serve important purposes. Vitamin C keeps your bones and teeth strong. Without it, your gums will bleed and your teeth will become loose and you may lose weight. Vitamin D also helps you to build strong bones. Children who don't get enough of it can suffer from curved spines and may not grow properly. Vitamin E deficiency diseases are rare. Since many foods contain this vitamin, almost everyone gets enough. Scientists are still not sure of the diseases caused by too little Vitamin E. Vitamin K helps our blood to clot. If you cut yourself, you need Vitamin K, since without it you would bleed for a long time.

? Questions

1. Read the sentence that follows: "Vitamins are a vital part of a person's diet; they are necessary to your health." What does the word *vital* mean?

   _____

   _____

2. Read the sentence that follows: "Most people get adequate vitamins from their food, so they do not need any vitamin pills." What does *adequate* mean?

   _____

   _____

3. Read the sentence that follows: "People who don't get enough vitamins may develop deficiency diseases." What is the meaning of the technical word *deficiency*?

   _____

   _____

4. Read the sentence that follows: "All of these people run the risk of not getting enough vitamins from their food, so they may need to take vitamin pills." What does the figurative phrase *run the risk of* mean?

   _____

   _____

5. Read the sentence that follows: "Vitamin A helps you see and it also keeps your skin healthy and fresh." What connotation does the word *fresh* add to the sentence?

   _____

   _____

✓ Answers

1. Read the sentence that follows: "Vitamins are a vital part of a person's diet; they are necessary to your health." What does the word *vital* mean? Vital *means "very important."*

This question requires students to use context clues to determine the word's meaning.

2. Read the sentence that follows: "Most people get adequate vitamins from their food, so they do not need any vitamin pills." What does *adequate* mean? Adequate *means "enough." This question also requires students to use context clues to determine the word's meaning.*

3. Read the sentence that follows: "People who don't get enough vitamins develop deficiency diseases." What is the meaning of the technical word *deficiency*? Deficiency *means "a lack of" something. Though this word has a technical meaning in the context of this topic, students can use context clues as well as their familiarity with the prefix* de- *to help them figure out the meaning of the word.*

4. Read the sentence that follows: "All of these people run the risk of not getting enough vitamins from their food, so they may need to take vitamin pills." What does the figurative phrase *run the risk of* mean? *The phrase means "may get." This question requires students to use context clues to determine the nonliteral meaning of the phrase.*

5. Read the sentence that follows: "Vitamin A helps you see and it also keeps your skin healthy and fresh." What connotation does the word *fresh* add to the sentence? *The word* fresh, *in this instance, suggests something positive about your face. A "fresh" face will look glowing and clean. This question requires students to be aware of language and how it impacts the tone of a passage.*

Extra practice

To help your child work on the skills assessed by this standard, try this activity:

1. Find an encyclopedia, either online or in book form, and have your child open it to a random page.

2. Ask your child to skim the page and point out any unfamiliar words or phrases. For each one, prompt your child to look for context clues to try to determine the meaning. If your child cannot determine the exact meaning, provide assistance. For example, you might start by discussing what the sentence is about. Then ask your child to make an educated guess about the meaning of the word or phrase.

3. Use a dictionary to check the definitions for all the unfamiliar words and phrases. Ask your child to make a list of all the new words and phrases he or she has encountered, along with their definitions.

Through this activity, your child will be directly practicing the skills covered by the standard. He or she will determine the meaning of words and phrases, including figurative, connotative, and technical meanings. Praise your child for this work, explaining exactly what skills have been used.

As you read with your child, practice these skills to figure out word meaning. Remind them of these steps:

1. Look for context clues. Begin with the adjacent words and phrases and then move to nearby phrases and sentences.
2. Visualize the word or what is being described to help put the word in context.
3. Look for root words. Are there words that sound or look similar to the unfamiliar word?
4. Consider the various meanings of multiple-meaning words. Does the first meaning that comes to mind make sense in the sentence?
5. Look for other places that an unfamiliar word is used. If it is used more than once in the text, the other places might help confirm its meaning.

Look for opportunities to further explore word meaning with your child. Encourage your child to use the word in a sentence. Or ask a question that helps your child relate the word to what he or she knows (e.g. "Have you heard the word *supplements* used before? If so, when?").

As children read, they will naturally build their vocabulary. Being able to use a variety of strategies to determine word meaning will help them meet the goals of the standard and be better readers across all disciplines.

 Quiz

Have your child read this passage and answer the questions that follow.

 Space Exploration

Humans have always looked to the stars for inspiration and guidance. For many centuries, different civilizations dreamed of what lay beyond the clouds, in the outer reaches of space. Finally, in the twentieth century, humans overcame countless obstacles and achieved one of the most amazing feats of all human history: not only were humans sent into space, but they also walked on the moon. However, since the 1970s, space exploration has taken a steady dive in priority and funding. Many people think that space exploration is simply too expensive. They argue that it is better to use that money to take care of problems on our own planet. I disagree.

Space exploration has already proven beneficial to humankind in so many ways. First, it has allowed us to study planets and other celestial bodies better. By placing equipment in space and on other planets, we can see more and get data that would be impossible to get from Earth. Second, many of the technologies created for space exploration have been used for products back on Earth. For example, did you know that handheld vacuum cleaners were first created for the space program? Finally, space exploration fills our need to learn about the vast world in which we live. Humans are naturally curious. If we abandon space exploration, we give up our sense of wonder and curiosity. Space exploration also gives us a goal to achieve—a goal that can unite all people and cultures.

I think we should create a space organization that brings together many different countries. The first goal should be to set up a habitat on the moon where scientists can live and study its properties. After that, we should create a ship that can carry astronauts to Mars and back. Explorers have dreamed of Mars for centuries, and it would be a monumental achievement for humans to finally set foot on the Red Planet.

❓ Questions

1. Read the sentence that follows: *Finally, in the twentieth century, humans overcame countless obstacles and achieved one of the most amazing feats of all human history: not only were humans sent into space, but they also walked on the moon.* What does the word *obstacles* mean as used in the sentence?

   _____

   _____

2. Read the sentence that follows: *However, since the 1970s, space exploration has taken a steady dive in priority and funding.* What does the word *priority* mean as used in the sentence?

   _____

   _____

3. Read the sentence that follows: *Space exploration has already proven beneficial to humankind in so many ways.* Does the writer use the word *beneficial* to reflect something positive or something negative? How do you know?

   _____

   _____

4. Read the sentence that follows: *If we abandon space exploration, we give up our sense of wonder and curiosity.* Does the writer use the word *abandon* to reflect something positive or something negative? How do you know?

   _____

   _____

5. Read the sentence that follows: *The first goal should be to set up a habitat on the moon where scientists can live and study its properties.* What does the word *habitat* mean as used in the sentence?

_____

_____

 **Answers**

1. Read the sentence that follows: *Finally, in the twentieth century, humans overcame countless obstacles and achieved one of the most amazing feats of all human history: not only were humans sent into space, but they also walked on the moon.* What does the word *obstacles* mean as used in the sentence? *The word means "challenges" or "difficulties."*

2. Read the sentence that follows: *However, since the 1970s, space exploration has taken a steady dive in priority and funding.* What does the word *priority* mean as used in the sentence? *The word means "importance."*

3. Read the sentence that follows: *Space exploration has already proven beneficial to humankind in so many ways.* Does the writer use the word *beneficial* to reflect something positive or something negative? How do you know? *The word* beneficial *is used to mean something positive. This is shown by the examples that are given, which are all positive things.*

4. Read the sentence that follows: *If we abandon space exploration, we give up our sense of wonder and curiosity.* Does the writer use the word *abandon* to reflect something positive or something negative? How do you know? *The word* abandon *is used to reflect something negative. This is shown by the fact that the author associates negative things with abandoning space exploration.*

5. Read the sentence that follows: *The first goal should be to set up a habitat on the moon where scientists can live and study its properties.* What does the word *habitat* mean as used in the sentence? *The word means "place to live."*

THE STANDARD

RL.6.1: *Supporting Evidence and Inferences – Literature*
Cite textual evidence to support analysis of what the text says explicitly as well as inferences drawn from the text.

What does it mean?

This literature standard focuses on a student's ability to comprehend what is stated in a passage and what can be inferred based on information in the text.

Try this together

Let's use the following story as an example of the kind of literature your child might encounter in school. To address this reading standard, a teacher might ask questions such as the ones that follow the story, or assign them as homework. We have provided possible answers in the "Answers" section, along with an explanation of how the questions connect to the standard.

Before trying this exercise with your child, read through the story and the questions that follow it. Then have your child read the story aloud to you and answer the questions. Talk about the answers together. Help your child realize that he or she can find answers to questions by looking back at the story for clues.

 ## A Rainy Day for Dante

It had been raining for almost a week. Dante was sick of TV, he was sick of Nintendo, and he didn't feel like reading any of his magazines. He looked at his rollerblades and rolled his eyes. "Just when I get what I want, the weather has to go against me," he said to himself. His grandfather had bought him the rollerblades for his birthday at the beginning of the week, but ever since, the rain hadn't stopped. All he could do was look at his gift.

"I'm so bored... bored," he muttered to himself.

His mother was at work and so was his older brother. He was left to take care of his sister Rosa. Sometimes Dante got along with Rosa; he would play "Horsey" with her and let her ride on his back, but sometimes he couldn't stand her. She wanted this, and she wanted that, and he didn't like to do everything for her.

Today was a school holiday, and both he and his sister were home from school. A whole day with nothing to do! After he got dressed, he fed Rosa and himself and then went back to his room to daydream.

Suddenly, he heard a sound outside his window. It was a high-pitched shrill noise and it was getting louder. Dante got up and went to the glass and looked out; he saw the strangest-looking cat with hardly any tail and ears that were pushed against its head. The animal was all wet and looked terrible.

"It looks so skinny. Maybe I should feed it," he thought to himself. He went into the kitchen where his sister's and his own cereal bowls sat on the counter waiting to be put in the sink and opened a cupboard where he found a can of tuna fish. He had heard that cats like fish, so he opened it up, and put some on a small dish.

Dante went to the back door and looked out at the cat, who was making that sound again—whining, and looking so sad and hungry. Dante opened the door and started out, but the cat backed away a bit and Dante stopped. He watched the cat and then slowly he put the plate on the porch very slowly. After a while, the cat moved forward, sniffed the food, and then hungrily devoured it.

Dante watched the food disappear before his eyes. When the cat was finished, it looked up at him. "You sure are one funny-looking cat," said Dante, who knelt down to pet the animal. It nudged its soaked body against him, anxious for attention. It felt good to touch the cat and hear it purr. A smile replaced the earlier frown on Dante's face. Suddenly, Dante was aware that the rain had stopped and the clouds were breaking. There was even a sliver of sun peeking out behind the gray. The cat rubbed against Dante one more time and then quickly ran down the steps and headed into a thicket behind the house while Dante stood, watching it go.

❓ Questions

1. Which sentence from the passage best tells why Dante was bored?

   _____

   _____

2. What does Dante think of his sister?

   _____

   _____

3. Analyze what the following sentences tell about Dante: "Dante opened the door and started out, but the cat backed away a bit and Dante stopped. He watched the cat and then he put the plate on the porch very slowly and stayed still. After a while, the cat moved forward, sniffed the food, and then hungrily devoured it."

   _____

   _____

4. How does the cat change Dante?

   _____

   _____

5. What can you infer Dante will most likely do once his mother comes home?

   _____

   _____

 **Answers**

1. Which sentence from the passage best tells why Dante was bored? *"It had been rain-ing for almost a week." This question requires students to find supporting evidence in the story. The reason that Dante is bored is not explicitly stated in the story, but the rain is a reasonable inference to make.*

2. What does Dante think of his sister? *Dante likes his sister, but that he gets tired of doing things for her. This requires students to analyze what is said about Dante and his sister. Students need to evaluate the evidence to make this judgment about what Dante thinks of her.*

3. Analyze what the following sentences reveal about Dante: "Dante opened the door and started out, but the cat backed away a bit and Dante stopped. He watched the cat, and then he put the plate on the porch very slowly and stayed still. After a while, the cat moved forward, sniffed the food, and then hungrily devoured it." *You can infer that Dante cares about animals and wants to help them. He is also aware of the cat's fears. Students will need to find evidence of what Dante's actions toward the cat mean in terms of his personality. This requires critical thinking.*

4. How does the cat change Dante? *Because of the cat, Dante forgot about being bored. Dante even smiled, which suggests he was happy. This question requires students to make an inference based on the evidence in the story.*

5. What can you infer Dante will most likely do once his mother comes home? *Answers may vary. Some students may say that Dante will go out and rollerblade now that the rain has stopped. Others might say that he'll do something with regard to the cat, for example, go looking for the cat, talk to his mother about the cat, decide to keep the cat, etc. This question requires students to make inferences based on the kind of person Dante is and the events that happen to him.*

Extra practice

To help your child work on the skills assessed by this standard, try this activity:

1. First ask your child to reread "A Rainy Day for Dante."
2. Then ask your child to choose a sentence that best support the inference that Dante was a responsible person.
3. Discuss the sentence that your child chooses and why it supports the inference. Ask if there are any other sentences that support this inference.

Through this activity, your child will be directly practicing the skills covered by the standard. He or she will find evidence to support an inference about the main character, a skill that requires critical judgment. Praise your child for this work, explaining exactly what skills have been used in this activity.

Have your child read this passage and write the answers independently in the space provided.

 Sam and Jimmy

Sam loved to sit on Jimmy's shoulder. He also loved to take little showers in the sink. Sam sang in the morning and the evening, and he flew in circles in the room, but Sam wasn't always this way.

When Jimmy first saw Sam, he was in a cage in a dark corner of a pet store and he didn't look very happy. The store was going out of business and Sam was on sale, so Jimmy begged his parents to buy him. After a short discussion, Jimmy's mom and dad decided a bird would make a good pet for Jimmy, so they brought Sam home. Sam had a nice new cage, much bigger than his old one, and he could look out the window and see birds and squirrels and trees and bushes. But Sam was strangely quiet, never making a sound.

This saddened Jimmy, but he would sit by the cage and talk to Sam anyway, often whistling to him and making bird sounds. He brought Sam special food and talked quietly to him. One night he dreamed that Sam jumped on his shoulder and sang softly in his ear.

Jimmy and his family went away on a trip and Sam was left in his cage under the care of a friend who came once a day to change his water and make sure he had enough to eat. When Jimmy got back, he opened the door of the cage. All of a sudden Sam flew onto his hand. Jimmy couldn't believe it. Then Sam started to sing a wonderful song. Jimmy couldn't have wished for a better homecoming.

Questions

1. Choose two sentences in the story that tell what Sam liked to do.

   _____

   _____

2. How did Sam change in the story?

   _____

   _____

3. What are three examples of evidence in the story that Jimmy loved Sam?

   _____

   _____

4. What inference can you make about Sam when Jimmy returns from his trip?

   _____

   _____

5. What is meant by the sentence "Jimmy couldn't have wished for a better homecoming"?

_____

_____

 **Answers**

Questions 1 and 2 require the student to find explicit evidence in the text. Questions 3 and 4 move students toward analyzing the story and identifying evidence in the story that supports an inference. Question 5 requires students to interpret the evidence in the story and then apply it.

1. Choose two sentences in the story tell what Sam liked to do. *"Sam loved to sit on Jimmy's shoulder; he also loved to take little showers in the sink." "Sam sang in the morning and the evening, and he flew in circles in the room, but Sam wasn't always this way."*

2. How did Sam change in the story? *When Jimmy first got Sam, Sam wouldn't sing. As the story moves forward, he begins to sing and act a lot happier.*

3. What are three examples of evidence in the text that Jimmy loved Sam? *Jimmy sat with Sam. He whistled to him and he gave him special food.*

4. What inference can you make about Sam after Jimmy returns from his trip? *You can infer that Sam truly missed Jimmy, based on the fact that he flies into his hand and greets him with a song.*

5. What is meant by the sentence "Jimmy couldn't have wished for a better homecoming"? *Coming home from his trip, Jimmy probably expected Sam to be the same as he was when he left. But because Sam had begun to sing, Jimmy's homecoming had turned into something beyond his expectations.*

THE STANDARD

RL.6.2: *Theme – Literature*
Determine a theme or central idea of a text and how it is conveyed through particular details; provide a summary of the text distinct from personal opinions or judgments.

What does it mean?

This literature standard focuses on a student's ability to analyze the theme, or lesson, of a story based on details, as well as to summarize the main events without allowing personal opinions or judgments to affect the summary.

Try this together

Let's use the following story as an example of the kind of literature your child might en-counter in school. To address this reading standard, a teacher might ask questions such as the ones that follow the story, or assign them as homework. We have provided possible answers in the "Answers" section, along with an explanation of how the questions connect to the standard.

Before trying this exercise with your child, read through the story and the questions that follow it. Then have your child read the passage aloud to you and answer the questions. Talk about the answers together. Help your child realize that he or she can find answers to questions by looking back at the passage for clues.

 ## Angela's Present

When Angela heard the doorbell ring, she opened the front door only to see a man driving a de-livery truck waving at her as he pulled away. She waved back and then looked down at the large package he had left. Her name was on the box that had her grandmother's return address. Three large words were written on the box: DO NOT OPEN. Angela brought the package into the house, shaking it to see what might be inside.

Angela put the package on the kitchen table and stared at it, then turned it around and around, looking at each side carefully. There were no clues, but she knew that anything from her grand-mother had to be good.

That evening her grandmother called. "Did you get my package, dear? You haven't opened it, have you?"

"Yes and no," laughed Angela, "yes, I got it; and no, I didn't open it."

Angela's grandmother made her promise not to open the box for a week, but she added that if Angela could figure out what was inside, she could open it sooner. Her grandmother said she would call every day to hear her guess.

Angela spent the whole next day trying to imagine what could fit inside the box. She knew it couldn't be a pet because it wouldn't be able to breathe in there for a week. The box was too small to hold the bike she had been asking for. When her grandmother called, she asked if it was a catcher's mitt, since she liked to play softball.

"Good guess," said her grandmother. "I'll call back tomorrow and see if you do any better."

The next day Angela thought of all the things she wanted. She went to a store and saw some attractive dresses that would just fit in the box. So when her grandmother called her, she asked her if it was a dress.

"Do you really want a dress?" asked her grandmother.

Angela said she wasn't sure. "Sorry, dear," answered Angela's grandmother, "I'll talk to you tomorrow."

Every day that week, Angela's grandmother called her to ask what was in the box, and every day, Angela had a new idea. Finally, she had only one more day. She needed to figure out what she really wanted, so she went to several stores in a mall nearby and studied every kind of merchandise she could find.

At last she found her way into a little shop that sold old clothes and jewelry. Tucked way back in an old jewelry case was a beautiful bracelet with stones of all different colors. When the light came through one of the stones, it made everything around it the color of the stone. To Angela, it was like magic; she knew quite suddenly that she wanted that bracelet more than anything she had ever wanted.

When her grandmother called, she held her breath. There was no way her grandmother could know about the bracelet, but, when she was told to guess, Angela asked if it was a bracelet. Her grandmother asked her if that was what she really wanted. When Angela said, "Yes, yes, that is what I really want," her grandmother told her to open her package.

Inside the box was a note: "My dearest Angela, if you truly know what you want, it shall be yours," it read.

Angela's grandmother said she would pick her up in the morning. They had some jewelry to buy.

❓ Questions

1. Which sentence from the story best suggests the theme?

   _____

   _____

   _____

2. Based on details in the story, what kind of person is Angela's grandmother?

   _____

   _____

   _____

3. What is one detail that would not be included in a summary of the story?

4. During the course of the story, what does Angela learn?

5. What does the grandmother teach Angela?

 **Answers**

1. *Which sentence from the story best suggests its theme?* "Inside the box was a note: 'My dearest Angela, if you truly know want you want, it shall be yours,' it read. This question requires students to first figure out what the theme of the story is and then find a sentence that suggests that theme.

2. Based on details in the story, what kind of person is Angela's grandmother? Based on her interactions with Angela, you can infer that the grandmother is loving, and also that she is fun-loving to have thought up this interesting way of presenting Angela's gift to her. This question requires student to think about details in the story that reveal hints about the grandmother's personality, especially her interactions with Angela.

3. What is one detail that would not be included in a summary of the story? Answers will vary, but should include any detail that is of minor importance to the story. Possible details include: the man driving the delivery truck waving at Angela; Angela putting the box on the kitchen table; the fact that the bracelet was tucked away in the back of a jewelry case. This question requires that students be able to distinguish between important details and minor, less important details.

4. During the course of the story, what does Angela learn? Angela learns that it is good to know what you really want; put another way, she learns that if you know what you really want, you'll be able to enjoy it more than anything else. This question requires that students analyze how the events of the story impact Angela.

5. What does the grandmother teach Angela? The grandmother teaches Angela to focus on what she wants and also how to be patient. This question requires that students focus on how the grandmother's scheme changes Angela's attitude about typical gift-giving.*

Extra practice

To help your child work on the skills assessed by this standard, try this activity:

1. First ask your child to reread the story.
2. Then ask your child to imagine Angela and her grandmother talking to each other while en route to the shop to buy the bracelet.
3. Ask your child to write down a short conversation between them that focuses on what Angela learned from her grandmother's actions.
4. Discuss the conversation and how it reflects the theme of the story.

Through this activity, your child will be directly practicing the skills covered by the standard. He or she will demonstrate a clear understanding of the theme and how it might be reflected by the characters' interactions. Praise your child for this work, explaining exactly what skills have been demonstrated.

Have your child read this passage and write the answers independently in the space provided.

 Lost Girl

It was about three in the afternoon when I found the horse. Her coat was matted with mud, but I could tell she was a fine animal underneath. She was standing on the side of the road, as if she were waiting for me. As I got nearer, she started looking a little nervous—rolling her eyes back and straightening out her ears—so I backed away. My grandfather had told me that the one thing you don't want to be near is a nervous horse. He used to be a farrier, which means that he hammered metal horseshoes onto horses' hooves.

When I got home, I told Grandpa about the horse and that we had to go find her. "What if she's hurt?" I asked.

Grandpa was reading in his chair, and he didn't even look up. "My horse wrangling days are over, Madeline," he said, but I begged and pleaded with him. I even made promises about how many extra farm chores I'd do. Finally, Grandpa gave in, and we went to find the mysterious horse.

The horse was just where I'd left her. "Stay in the truck, Madeline," Grandpa said. I watched as he slowly approached the horse and began to talk to her—well, not talk exactly, but I knew he was whispering to the horse, making her feel at ease like when you make nice small-talk with someone you just met. The horse seemed to respond and soon he walked her into the trailer and we brought her home. We named her Lost Girl.

We cleaned Lost Girl up, and Grandpa put new horseshoes on her. We kept her in an old tractor shed, but I never rode her because we didn't have a saddle. Still, I went down every day to feed and brush her, and I even put a harness on her and trotted her around the yard. Sometimes I snuck down at night, too, and I'd pat her side and say her name. I'd listen to her breathing with the music of the crickets in the background.

Then, just as I had convinced Grandpa to borrow a neighbor's old saddle and start giving me riding lessons, I saw something terrible. We were in town at the supermarket, and I noticed a flyer near the checkout. "Lost Horse," it said in large letters, with a picture of Lost Girl. I gasped out loud. Grandpa came over and asked what I was looking at.

Even though part of me knew it would mean I would lose Lost Girl, I pointed at the sign, my hand shaking. "That's probably not her, though," I said. "Her ears are different. They are very different," I protested.

I told my grandpa that we had to keep Lost Girl. He just kept on loading the groceries in the back of the truck, not saying a word. "She must not have liked it where she was," I insisted. Can you think of something you really wanted for your birthday so badly that it hurt? I wanted to keep Lost Girl ten times more than I'd ever wanted anything else in my whole life.

But, when we got home, Grandpa called the number on the flyer. Within an hour, a family from Aurora arrived at the house. I couldn't bear to go outside to meet them. Instead, I watched from the window as they led Lost Girl away. Their little girl was crying because she was so happy. I wish I could say that seeing her made me forget how angry I was. I should have realized that Lost Girl was her horse and hers to take, but I didn't. Even though I had my friends at school and my mom and dad and grandfather, I felt totally alone.

? Questions

1. What do you think that Madeline learned from the events of the story? Use details from the story to support your answer.

   _____

   _____

   _____

2. What detail is not important to a summary of the story?

   _____

   _____

3. What are three details that should be included in a summary?

   _____

   _____

   _____

4. What event in the story most impacts its theme?

   _____

   _____

5. What sentence from the story best suggests its theme?

   _____

   _____

 **Answers**

Question 1 requires students to examine a character's behavior in the face of events, which often suggests the theme of a story. Questions 2 and 3 require student to distinguish between important and minor, less important, details in a story. evaluate the events and details in a story so that only the important details are included. Questions 4 and 5 require that students analyze the story in light of the theme that is suggested.

1. What do you think that Madeline learns from the events of the story? Use details from the story to support your answer. *She learns that even if it hurts, you need to do the right thing.*

2. What detail is not important to a summary of the story? *Answers will vary, but should include any detail that is of minor importance to the story. Possible details include: Madeline found Lost Girl in the afternoon; Grandpa unloaded groceries from the car; Madeline did not have a saddle.*

3. What are three details that should be included in a summary? *Answers will vary. However, a good summary would probably include: Madeline found a horse; Madeline took care of the horse; Madeline saw a note about a horse that was lost.*

4. What event in the story most impacts its theme? *The owners taking Lost Girl away from Madeline.*

5. What sentence from the story best suggests its theme? *Accept answers that can be well-supported by the story. Possible answer: "Even though I had my friends at school and my mom and dad and grandfather, I felt totally alone."*

THE STANDARD

RL.6.3: *Plot and Character – Literature*
Describe how a particular story's or drama's plot unfolds in a series of episodes as well as how the characters respond or change as the plot moves toward a resolution.

What does it mean?

This literature standard focuses on a student's ability to analyze the plot of a passage and the events that move the story forward, as well as understand how characters react to these events and possibly change as a result of what happens in the plot.

Try this together

Let's use the following story as an example of the kind of literature your child might encounter in school. To address this reading standard, a teacher might ask questions such as the ones that follow the story, or assign them as homework. We have provided possible answers in the "Answers" section, along with an explanation of how the questions connect to the standard.

Before trying this exercise with your child, read through the story and the questions that follow it. Then have your child read the passage aloud to you and answer the questions. Talk about the answers together. Help your child realize that she can find answers to questions by looking back at the story for clues.

 ## My Friend Nick

The first time I saw my friend Nick, he was late for the school bus. It was the first day of school and I was just getting on when I saw him running down the street, so I put my foot on the step of the bus and stayed on the sidewalk, explaining to the bus driver that someone was coming.

Nick was always late; I guess he couldn't help himself. It might seem strange for us to be friends, because I am twelve and Nick is only nine. He was in the second grade and I was in fifth grade when we first met. He was my next-door neighbor, though, so I felt like I should watch out for him, but I am getting ahead of myself.

We saw each other at lunch once in awhile, and sometimes at recess. After school, we would often see each other hanging around in our neighborhood or at the park.

At first we'd just call out to each other, "Hi, Gloria!" and "Hey, Nick!" Our parents knew each other, though, and they would always talk while we played.

After awhile, it seemed only natural to spend time with Nick. He started coming over after school to play computer games at my apartment. Nick was really proficient at computer games, and I couldn't keep up with him. He had great eye-hand coordination and he had a real understanding of the games.

But Nick had some other problems. Nick didn't like school much, and he had a lot of trouble reading. I first realized that when I was fooling around on the computer between games, sending instant messages and e-mails back and forth. Nick was there, too, and he kept interrupting to ask what I was writing. I realized then that he couldn't read what was on the screen because we used a lot of words that he didn't know.

I have always loved to read, and I have a big collection of books. I was sad that Nick had such difficulty reading and hoped I could help him out. Maybe then he wouldn't always be so late for the school bus, I thought.

One afternoon, I decided to ask Nick if he would like to read a book with me. At first, he hesitated, but I reminded him of how much he had taught me about computer games, so he agreed.

I picked something easy, although I don't remember exactly what it was, but I do remember that we sat together and read the words together. At first, Nick read very slowly, and he would stop a lot for help. After a little while, though, he started to get excited about it, and he was getting into the story and even began to recognize some of the difficult words.

We started to read together almost every afternoon. We made it a game to see who could read the fastest. Of course, I usually let him win. I felt like a big sister to him after all that time. Besides, I want to become a teacher one day, so this was a great way to practice.

Well, what do you know, Nick started to read by himself, too, and he was really into it. I was also pleased to notice that he started to arrive on time for the school bus. It made me feel good to see him look so much happier when I saw him in the halls at school. I guess that's what teaching—and friendship—are all about.

Questions

1. Why did Gloria want to help Nick?

   _____

   _____

2. Why is Nick at first hesitant to read with Gloria?

   _____

   _____

3. How does Gloria's helping Nick influence the plot?

   _____

   _____

4. Read the sentence from the story: *I was also pleased to notice that he started to arrive on time for the school bus.* What does this show about Nick?

   _____

   _____

5. At the end of the story, why does Gloria feel good?

_____

_____

 **Answers**

1. *Why did Gloria want to help Nick?* *She felt sorry for him because he couldn't read well and because he was late to school. This question requires students to analyze the reasons for Gloria's actions according to the information in the story.*

2. *Why is Nick at first hesitant to read with Gloria?* *You can infer that Nick was embarrassed that he could not read well. This question requires students to make an inference based on the clues in the story.*

3. *How does Gloria's helping Nick influence the plot?* *The plot changes when Gloria starts to help Nick because it helps Nick to change. This question requires students to think about the impact of a particular event on the development of the story.*

4. *Read the sentence from the story: "I was also pleased to notice that he started to arrive on time for the school bus." What does this show about Nick?* *You can infer that this means Nick is on time because likes school more. This question requires students to analyze a sentence and make an inference about a character based on it.*

5. *At the end of the story, why does Gloria feel good?* *Gloria is glad about the fact that she has helped Nick become a better reader. She also realizes that this is what being a teacher, and a friend, is all about. This question requires students to analyze a character based on the character's thoughts and reactions to events.*

Extra practice

To help your child work on the skills assessed by this standard, try this activity:

1. First ask your child to reread "My Friend Nick."
2. Explain that your child will now make a story map, showing the main events in the story.
3. Have your child make a map consisting of five event boxes. Have your child write descriptions of the events in the box.
4. Then discuss with your child how these events affected or changed the main characters.

Through this activity, your child will be directly practicing the skills covered by the standard. He or she will determine how a plot develops through events and how characters respond or change because of the events. Praise your child for this work, explaining exactly what skills were used in this activity.

 Quiz

Have your child read this story and write the answers independently in the space provided.

 Ethan's First Job

It was still dark outside when Ethan and his father arrived at Mr. Fletcher's cabin. They hitched their wagon to the rail and their horse drank deeply of the water that was provided. They could see the candles burning inside the cabin. Ethan was excited about his first job away from his family's farm. He remembered how he had begged Mr. Fletcher to let him help out on his farm.

"I'm twelve years old and I can work hard. I'll help you plow those weeds from your corn. I've done it with father many a time." Mr. Fletcher was a bit doubtful, but he had agreed to pay Ethan to live and work on his farm this month and Ethan was eager to prove his worth.

The door to the log cabin opened, and Mr. Fletcher greeted the man and boy. "It's time to feed and milk," he told Ethan, who was used to doing these chores. As his father turned his horse toward home, Ethan had just enough time for a pang of homesickness, but then, Mr. Fletcher's strong arms hurried the boy along toward the barn. Ethan threw plump yellow grains of corn to the chickens, while the older man milked Lilyanne, the cow.

As the sun began to rise, Mr. Fletcher hitched his two mules, Corrie and Bess, to the lines that connected the animals to the plow, and then the farmer told Ethan to sit down on the sack of straw behind the mules and to guide the animals by holding onto the lines. The boy was instructed to keep the mules moving at a steady pace and to prevent them from trampling the corn. Mr. Fletcher took his own place behind the plow. Its sharp iron blades would rip up the weeds between the neat rows of corn.

"C'mon Corrie, Bess," Mr. Fletcher said in a kind, calm voice. The plow moved steadily through the cornfield. Halfway down the second row of corn, the plow hit a rock and Mr. Fletcher called to his mules, "Whoa! Back up, Bess. Back, Corrie. That's good." The farmer shook the plow up and down until the iron blades became free again. Luckily, the blades were not damaged.

As the plow began to move again, Ethan shook the line to get the mules to move faster. When Corrie stumbled on another rock, the boy shouted, "Get up!" and tapped her hard with the line. Corrie jumped with surprise and then began running through the field. Bess had no choice but to keep up with her. The two mules stomped the corn and kicked against the plow. Ethan tried to stop them by pulling on the lines, but it did no good. Mr. Fletcher, Ethan, and the plow were getting dragged along through the cornfield. Mr. Fletcher shouted, "Whoa" till he was hoarse, but the mules didn't stop until they got to the end of the field and then, they quietly began eating grass.

Mr. Fletcher was furious. He grabbed Ethan by the arm and held it in a tight grip. "Son," he said, "don't you ever hit my mules again. I have a mind to send you home right now!"

Ethan pulled away, his face hot with embarrassment. "I'm sorry," he said in a small voice. "I didn't mean to hurt them." The boy's head hung down as he walked away slowly.

"Wait!" Mr. Fletcher shouted. "Do you think you can learn to drive these mules properly?"

"I'll try, Mr. Fletcher," Ethan said, sniffling a bit. "I promise."

"Well, then do what I do. Talk easy and soft to Bess and Corrie, and don't get them riled up."

Ethan pulled back on the lines gently and spoke in a soft voice. The mules walked slowly back to the corn rows, pulling the plow behind them. The farmer maneuvered the plow to cut the weeds out of the soil. As Ethan got more confident, his mind wandered a bit. He began to think of how he would spend the money he earned with Mr. Fletcher. Maybe he would buy some chickens and sell the eggs. He might even make enough money to buy himself a pony someday, now that he was a working man.

Questions

1. Read the sentence from the story: "As his father turned his horse toward home, Ethan had just enough time for a pang of homesickness, but then, Mr. Fletcher's strong arms hurried the boy along toward the barn." What does this sentence suggest about Ethan?

   _____

   _____

2. Which event most propels, or moves, the plot forward?

   _____

   _____

3. Why is Mr. Fletcher upset with Ethan when the mules run off?

   _____

   _____

4. Read the sentence that follows: "'Do you think you can learn to drive these mules properly?'" What does this suggest about Mr. Fletcher?

   _____

   _____

5. How does Ethan change in the course of the story?

   _____

   _____

 Answers

Questions 1 and 4 require the student to interpret the information in the story to infer character reactions. Question 2 requires students to analyze the events of the story and decide which ones more greatly impact the plot. Question 3 requires students to recount a central event in the story. Question 5 requires students to analyze the changes in a character.

1. Read the sentence from the story: "As his father turned his horse toward home, Ethan had just enough time for a pang of homesickness, but then, Mr. Fletcher's strong arms hurried the boy along toward the barn." What does this sentence suggest about Ethan? *It suggests that Ethan isn't as sure of himself as he first seems and is still very attached to the security of being with his family.*

2. Which event most propels, or moves, the plot forward? *The event that propels the plot the most is Ethan's talking loudly to the mules and hitting one with the line.*

3. Why is Mr. Fletcher upset with Ethan when the mules run off? *Mr. Fletcher is upset because Ethan almost ruined the plow and upset the mules.*

4. Read the sentence that follows: "Do you think you can learn to drive these mules properly?" What does this suggest about Mr. Fletcher? *This suggests that Mr. Fletcher has a softer side and is willing to give Ethan a second chance.*

5. How does Ethan change in the course of the story? *At the beginning of the story, Ethan seems sure that he knows how to do his job. But after realizing he had done something bad, he apologizes and starts to follow Mr. Fletcher's instructions; he then understands that he doesn't know everything.*

THE STANDARD

RL.6.4: *Vocabulary – Literature*
Determine the meaning of words and phrases as they are used in a text, including figurative and connotative meanings; analyze the impact of a specific word choice on meaning and tone.

What does it mean?

This literature standard focuses on a student's ability to comprehend words and phrases in a literary work, including words and phrases that are used figuratively, as well as to understand the connotation (or associated meaning) of words and phrases. It also requires that students analyze how a specific word impacts the meaning and tone of a passage.

Try this together

Let's use the following story as an example of the kind of literature your child might encounter in school. To address this learning standard, a teacher might ask questions such as the ones that follow the story, or assign them as homework. We have provided possible answers in the "Answers" section, along with an explanation of how the questions connect to the standard.

Before trying this exercise with your child, read through the story and the questions that follow it. Then have your child read the story aloud to you and answer the questions. Talk about the answers together. Help your child realize that he or she can find answers to questions by looking back at the passage for clues.

Excerpt from *Jo's Boys* by Louisa May Alcott

'Mother dear, I didn't say anything till it was sure because it would only worry you; but Aunt Jo and I have been on the look-out for it some time, and now it has come. You know her publisher, Mr. Tiber, is one of the most successful men in the business; also generous, kind, and the soul of honor—as his treatment of Aunty proves. Well, I've rather hankered for that place; for I love books, and as I can't make them I'd like to publish them. That needs some literary taste and judgment, it brings you in contact with fine people, and is an education in itself. Whenever I go into that large, handsome room to see Mr. Tiber for Aunt Jo, I always want to stay; for its lined with books and pictures, famous men and women come and go, and Mr. Tiber sits at his desk like a sort of king, receiving his subjects; for the greatest authors are humble to him, and wait his Yes or No with anxiety. Of course I've nothing to do with all that, and may never have; but I like to see it, and the atmosphere is so different from the dark offices and hurly-burly of many other trades, where nothing but money is talked about, that it seems another world, and I feel at home in it. Yes, I'd rather beat the door-mats and make fires there than be head clerk in the great hide and leather store at a big salary.' Here Demi paused for breath; and Mrs. Meg, whose face had been growing brighter and brighter, exclaimed eagerly:

'Just what I should like! Have you got it? Oh, my dear boy! your fortune is made if you go to that well-established and flourishing place, with those good men to help you along!'

❓ Questions

1. Read the sentence that follows: "'You know her publisher, Mr. Tiber, is one of the most successful men in the business; also generous, kind, and the soul of honor—as his treatment of Aunty proves.'" What does the phrase *soul of honor* mean?

   _____

   _____

2. Read the sentence that follows: "'Well, I've rather hankered for that place; for I love books, and as I can't make them I'd like to publish them.'" What does *hankered* mean?

   _____

   _____

3. Read the sentence that follows: "'Whenever I go into that large, handsome room to see Mr. Tiber for Aunt Jo, I always want to stay; for its lined with books and pictures, famous men and women come and go, and Mr. Tiber sits at his desk like a sort of king, receiving his subjects; for the greatest authors are humble to him, and wait his Yes or No with anxiety.'" What connotation does the word *handsome* have?

   _____

   _____

   _____

4. Read the sentence that follows: "'Of course I've nothing to do with all that, and may never have; but I like to see it, and the atmosphere is so different from the dark offices and hurly-burly of many other trades, where nothing but money is talked about, that it seems another world, and I feel at home in it.'" How does the term *hurly-burly* impact the tone of the story?

   _____

   _____

   _____

5. Read the sentence that follows: "'Oh, my dear boy! your fortune is made if you go to that well-established and flourishing place, with those good men to help you along!'" What does *flourishing* mean in this sentence?

_____

_____

 **Answers**

1. Read the sentence that follows: "'You know her publisher, Mr. Tiber, is one of the most successful men in the business; also generous, kind, and the soul of honor—as his treatment of Aunty proves.'" What does the phrase *soul of honor* mean? *This figurative phrase means "very honest," based on the context of the sentence. This question requires students to analyze the context clues near the expression and use them to understand the figurative phrase's meaning.*

2. Read the sentence that follows: "'Well, I've rather hankered for that place; for I love books, and as I can't make them I'd like to publish them.'" What does *hankered* mean? *It means "wanted," based on the context provided. This question again requires students to use context clues to determine the word's meaning.*

3. Read the sentence that follows: "'Whenever I go into that large, handsome room to see Mr. Tiber for Aunt Jo, I always want to stay; for its lined with books and pictures, famous men and women come and go, and Mr. Tiber sits at his desk like a sort of king, receiving his subjects; for the greatest authors are humble to him, and wait his Yes or No with anxiety.'" What connotation does the word *handsome* have? *The word* handsome *suggests a place that is good-looking or well-appointed. This question requires students to analyze the various connotations of a word and recognize the association one has with the word.*

4. Read the sentence that follows: "'Of course I've nothing to do with all that, and may never have; but I like to see it, and the atmosphere is so different from the dark offices and hurly-burly of many other trades, where nothing but money is talked about, that it seems another world, and I feel at home in it.'" How does the term *hurly-burly* impact the tone of the story? *The term* hurly-burly *sets the tone for these establishments as being busy in a rather negative sense, rather than being busy in a positive sense. This question requires students to be aware of language and how it impacts the tone of a story.*

5. Read the sentence that follows: "'Oh, my dear boy! your fortune is made if you go to that well-established and flourishing place, with those good men to help you along!'" What does *flourishing* mean in this sentence? Flourishing *means "successful" as used in the sentence. This question requires students to study the context of a sentence and figure out the meaning of a word.*

Extra practice

To help your child work on the skills assessed by this standard, try this activity:

1. First ask your child to reread the excerpt from *Jo's Boys.*
2. Then ask your child to choose three of the vocabulary words and write a sentence using each one.
3. Have your child read the sentences aloud.
4. Then discuss what the words mean and if they fit into the sentences correctly.

Through this activity, your child will be directly practicing the skills covered by the standard. Praise your child for this work, explaining exactly what skills were used in this activity.

Have your child read this passage and write the answers independently in the space provided.

Excerpt from *Jo's Boys* (cont'd.)

'I think I have, but we mustn't be too sure of anything yet. I may not suit; I'm only on trial, and must begin at the beginning and work my way up faithfully. Mr. Tiber was very kind, and will push me on as fast as is fair to the other fellows, and as I prove myself fit to go up. I'm to begin the first of next month in the book-room, filling orders; and I go round and get orders, and do various other things of the sort. I like it. I am ready to do anything about books, if it's only to dust them,' laughed Demi, well pleased with his prospects, for, after trying various things, he seemed at last to have found the sort of work he liked, and a prospect that was very inviting to him.

'You inherit that love of books from grandpa; he can't live without them. I'm glad of it. Tastes of that kind show a refined nature, and are both a comfort and a help all one's life. I am truly glad and grateful, John, that at last you want to settle, and have got such an entirely satisfactory place. Most boys begin much earlier; but I don't believe in sending them out to face the world so young, just when body and soul need home care and watchfulness. Now you are a man, and must begin your life for yourself. Do your best, and be as honest, useful, and happy as your father, and I won't care about making a fortune.'

'I'll try, mother. Couldn't have a better chance; for Tiber & Co. treat their people like gentlemen, and pay generously for faithful work. Things are done in a businesslike way there, and that suits me. I hate promises that are not kept, and shiftless or tyrannical ways anywhere. Mr. Tiber said: "This is only to teach you the ropes, Brooke; I shall have other work for you by and by." Aunty told him I had done book notices, and had rather a fancy for literature; so though I can't produce any "works of Shakespeare", as she says, I may get up some little things later. If I don't, I think it a very honorable and noble profession to select and give good books to the world; and I'm satisfied to be a humble helper in the work.'

'I'm glad you feel so. It adds so much to one's happiness to love the task one does. I used to hate teaching; but housekeeping for my own family was always sweet, though much harder in many ways. Isn't Aunt Jo pleased about all this?' asked Mrs. Meg, already seeing in her mind's eye a splendid sign with 'Tiber, Brooke & Co.' over the door of a famous publishing house.

? Questions

1. Read the sentence that follows: "'I may not suit; I'm only on trial, and must begin at the beginning and work my way up faithfully.'" What does the word *suit* mean as used in the sentence?

    _____

    _____

2. Read the sentence that follows: "'Tastes of that kind show a refined nature, and are both a comfort and a help all one's life. I am truly glad and grateful, John, that at last you want to settle, and have got such an entirely satisfactory place.'" What connotation does the word *satisfactory* have as used in the sentence?

    _____

    _____

3. Read the sentence that follows: "'Aunty told him I had done book notices, and had rather a fancy for literature; so though I can't produce any "works of Shakespeare", as she says, I may get up some little things later.'" What is the meaning of the word *fancy* as used in the sentence?

    _____

    _____

4. Read the sentence that follows: "'If I don't, I think it a very honorable and noble profession to select and give good books to the world; and I'm satisfied to be a humble helper in the work.'" What impact does the word *humble* have on the tone of the story?

    _____

    _____

5. Read the sentence that follows: "'Isn't Aunt Jo pleased about all this?' asked Mrs. Meg, already seeing in her mind's eye a splendid sign with 'Tiber, Brooke & Co.' over the door of a famous publishing house.'" What does the figurative phrase *in her mind's eye* mean?

    _____

    _____

✓ Answers

Questions 1 and 3 require the student to interpret the context clues to figure out the meaning of the unknown words. Question 2 requires students to analyze the connotations that a word has. Question 4 requires students to analyze the impact of a word on the meaning or tone of the text. Question 5 requires students to analyze the meaning of a figurative phrase through context clues.

1. Read the sentence that follows: "'I may not suit; I'm only on trial, and must begin at the beginning and work my way up faithfully.'" What does the word *suit* mean as used in the sentence? *The word means "not be good enough" in this context.*

2. Read the sentence that follows: "'Tastes of that kind show a refined nature, and are both a comfort and a help all one's life. I am truly glad and grateful, John, that at last you want to settle, and have got such an entirely satisfactory place.'" What connotation does the word *satisfactory* have as used in the sentence? *The connotation of* satisfactory *is that the company is a very good one. It has a positive connotation.*

3. Read the sentence that follows: "'Aunty told him I had done book notices, and had rather a fancy for literature; so though I can't produce any "works of Shakespeare", as she says, I may get up some little things later.'" What is the meaning of the word *fancy* as used in the sentence? *The word* fancy *has more than one meaning, but context tells the reader that it means "like" as it is used in the sentence.*

4. Read the sentence that follows: "'If I don't, I think it a very honorable and noble profession to select and give good books to the world; and I'm satisfied to be a humble helper in the work.'" What impact does the word *humble* have on the tone of the story? *The word* humble *as it is positioned creates a tone of down to earthiness and humility and tells the reader what kind of person Demi is.*

5. Read the sentence that follows: "'Isn't Aunt Jo pleased about all this?' asked Mrs. Meg, already seeing in her mind's eye a splendid sign with 'Tiber, Brooke & Co.' over the door of a famous publishing house.'" What does the figurative phrase *in her mind's eye* mean? *This phrase means that Aunt Jo is imagining a sign; she sees it in her mind's eye, which does not exist in a literal way.*

THE STANDARD

W.6.1: *Writing Arguments*
Write arguments to support claims with clear reasons and relevant evidence.
W 6.1.a: *Introduce claim(s) and organize the reasons and evidence clearly.*
W 6.1.b: *Support claim(s) with clear reasons and relevant evidence, using credible sources and demonstrating an understanding of the topic or text.*
W 6.1c: *Use words, phrases, and clauses to clarify the relationships among claim(s) and reasons.*
W 6.1d: *Establish and maintain a formal style.*
W 6.1e: *Provide a concluding statement or section that follows from the argument presented.*

What does it mean?

This standard focuses on a child's ability to write a well-organized paragraph or series of paragraphs. It is designed to assess how well a child can develop a topic by providing appropriate supporting information and make connections between and among the ideas.

The focus of this writing standard is writing an opinion, or claim. Opinion pieces are defined as those in which the writer develops a logical, well-supported argument or claim based on appropriate reasons and evidence. Sometimes referred to as persuasive writing, these pieces attempt to convince the reader that the ideas and opinions presented are worth adopting.

As shown in the sub-steps of the W.6.1 writing standard, the writing assesses the basic elements of a paragraph or essay, including the introduction (W.6.1a), body (W.6.1.b), and conclusion (W.6.1.e). It also focuses on using words, phrases, and clauses to clarify relationships among claims and reasons (W.6.1.c) and establishing and maintaining a formal style (W.6.1.d).

Try this together

Regardless of their skill level, all writers get better with practice. Unfortunately, many young writers become overwhelmed when writing is taught all at once. It may help to break down the writing process and focus on one part of the W.6.1 standard at a time. We will look at how this might be done.

Here's a writing prompt similar to one that might be used to test this standard. We have provided a sample answer, along with an explanation of how it all connects to the standard.

 ## Prompt

Evidence points to the fact that Americans are exercising less and are in much poorer physical condition than earlier generations. Some people blame computers and television for keeping young people from being outdoors exercising or playing sports. Some people believe that requiring sports in schools on a daily basis would help solve the problem. Write a short opinion essay in which you explain your views about this topic. Be sure to include reasons and evidence to support your view.

After reading the prompt, have your child to write a topic sentence that states the opinion he or she wants to present.

Next, ask your child to think of reasons and evidence that will help convince readers that the opinion presented makes sense. As your child writes about the reasons and evidence in the body of the essay, encourage him or her to use words, phrases, and clauses that connect ideas.

Finally, have your child write a concluding statement. Explain that the conclusion should sum up the main opinion presented in the essay. It should not introduce new ideas.

 ## Sample Answer

I believe that schools should require gym or sports daily because students are not getting enough exercise. Years ago, before the era of computers, kids played outside a lot more than they do now, playing games and running around. This kept kids in good shape.

Now I notice that most of my classmates are not in good shape, and a good number of them are overweight. It seems obvious that this is the result of pastimes that do not require physical activity, such as computer games and computer time in general. Some of these same classmates make poor food choices as well, which makes the problem worse.

Although some students my age say that exercise is a personal decision and schools shouldn't concern themselves with what we do or do not do, I feel that teaching kids how to get and stay in shape should be part of the educational process.

For these reasons, I think that it would be a good step for schools to require students to do more in terms of daily exercise. This would benefit them, even if they don't like the idea.

What's the point?

The main goal of this standard is to encourage students to formulate opinions and back them up with reasons and evidence. Note how in the sample answer, the student provides reasons why many classmates are not in good shape. This helps support the idea that schools should require students to participate in daily exercise. Simply stating *"I believe that schools should require gym or sports daily"* would not be sufficient for this standard, because it's a claim that lacks support.

Also note how the student presented an opposing opinion in the paragraph that begins "Although some students . . . " Many opinion essays do this, as it is an effective way to counter an opposing claim.

Finally, note that the last paragraph contains a concluding sentence that sums up the claim presented in the essay.

Extra practice

To help your child work on the skills assessed by this standard, try this activity:

1. Have your child think of an issue in the world about which he or she has a strong opinion. Brainstorm with your child and help them decide if the issue they want to explore is something local (for example, traffic problems in your community) or something nation- or worldwide (for example, the need for mutual respect among nations).
2. Ask your child to draft a topic sentence that states the opinion or claim.
3. Then have your child make a list of reasons that support his or her opinion on this issue. Help them draft a 2-3 sentence paragraph for each reason listed.
4. Finally, help your child draft a final paragraph that contains a concluding sentence.
5. Together, read through the draft and note places where the argument might be improved or more clearly stated.

Through this activity, your child will be directly practicing the skills covered by the standard. He or she will experience first-hand how an opinion can become a well-supported argument. Praise your child for this work, explaining exactly what skills were used in the activity.

 Quiz

In this quiz, your child will be asked to write an opinion essay. You will need to read the essay and decide how well your child has addressed the writing prompt.

 **Prompt**

The Internet provides access to all kinds of information. Some of it may not be suitable for young people. Some people believe that there should be some way to regulate the Internet. Others believe just the opposite. What is your opinion about regulating information on the Internet?

Be sure to:

- Introduce your claim.
- Support your claim with reasons and evidence.
- Use words, phrases, and clauses to clarify the relationships among claim(s) and reasons.
- Establish and maintain a formal style.
- Provide a concluding statement or section that follows from the argument presented.

_____

_____

_____

_____

_____

_____

_____

_____

_____

_____

_____

THE STANDARD

W.6.5: Planning and Revising
With some guidance and support from peers and adults, develop and strengthen writing as needed by planning, revising, editing, rewriting, or trying a new approach. (Editing for conventions should demonstrate command of Language standards 1-3 up to and including grade 6.)

What does it mean?

This writing standard focuses on a child's ability to improve upon his or her writing. The standard includes strategies for planning one's writing, as well as for revising the writing to make it clearer. The standard also focuses on editing for punctuation, spelling, grammar, and other writing conventions. As such, it is closely related to the Conventions of Standard English standards that are part of the Common Core Language skills. The sixth grade standards related to this are highlighted in the sidebar.

L.6.1: Demonstrate command of the conventions of standard English grammar and usage when writing or speaking.

- *L.6.1.a:* Ensure that pronouns are in the proper case (subjective, objective, possessive).
- *L.6.1.b:* Use intensive pronouns (e.g., myself, ourselves).
- *L.6.1.c:* Recognize and correct inappropriate shifts in pronoun number and person.
- *L.6.1.d:* Recognize and correct vague pronouns (i.e., ones with unclear or ambiguous antecedents).
- *L.6.1.e:* Recognize variations from standard English in their own and others' writing and speaking, and identify and use strategies to improve expression in conventional language.

L.6.2: Demonstrate command of the conventions of standard English capitalization, punctuation, and spelling when writing.

- *L.6.2.a:* Use punctuation (commas, parentheses, dashes) to set off nonrestrictive/parenthetical elements.
- *L.6.2.b:* Spelling correctly.

Try this together

In the previous lesson, you helped your child plan a piece of writing. This lesson will focus on the revising and editing stages of writing.

Explain that writing involves several steps. The revision process is when a writer looks back at the draft to improve upon it. Revising involves reading it to make sure that the central idea is clearly stated; that there are facts, definitions, and details supporting the central idea; that the organization makes sense; and that there is no extraneous information. Writers should also look for vague or overused words during the revision process to see if they can find other options.

Once all revisions have taken place, the draft is ready to be edited. It is during the editing process that a writer checks to make sure that the grammar, spelling, punctuation, and other language conventions are correct.

A checklist like the one on the following page can help your child revise and edit any piece of writing.

Before your child revises and edits the following paragraph, read through and familiarize yourself with the errors it contains. This will make it easier for you to be of assistance. Encourage your son or daughter to mark the paragraph while looking for ways to improve it. This can be done by circling or underlining certain parts of the text. Also suggest that the paragraph be read through several times to make sure that all errors are caught.

 ## Plastic Water Bottles

> We all need to stop buy and use plastic bottles of water. Plastic is'nt good for the enviroment. Because plastic isn't biodegradable, anything maid from it just sits around in landfills and garbage dumps for a long long time instead of drinking water from plastic bottles, we shoud use tap water more often.

 ## Answers

Note that certain revision changes, such as the concluding sentence, will vary from person to person. This exercise requires your child to make revisions and edits based on his or her understanding of clear and appropriate language usage. It also requires your child to understand the basic organization of an argument, with an introductory topic sentence that states an opinion, supporting details in the body, and a concluding sentence that sums up the central idea. Corrected paragraph:

We all need to stop buying and using plastic bottles of water. Plastic isn't good for the environment. Because plastic isn't biodegradable, anything made from it just sits around in landfills and garbage dumps for a long, long time. Instead of drinking water from plastic bottles, we should use tap water more often. If we all changed our habits and stopped buying and using plastic bottles of water, we'd be helping to improve the world for ourselves and for generations to come.

Extra practice

To help your child work on the skills assessed by this standard, try this activity:

Students tend to think that a piece of writing is finished once the last sentence has been written, but good writers continuously go back to improve what they've written, revising each sentence until their writing expresses ideas clearly and convincingly.

1. Explain to your child that he or she is now going to take the paragraph on plastic water bottles and revise it by turning it into a three-paragraph essay. The first paragraph should focus on the opinion, or claim. The second paragraph should give reasons and evidence of why the claim makes sense. The third paragraph should sum up the main opinion of the essay.

2. Allow your child time to make all revisions he or she thinks are necessary. Encourage him or her to look at the Revising and Editing Checklist provided in this book.

Through this activity, your child will be directly practicing the skills covered by the standard. He or she will learn about the importance of revising and editing as a way of strengthening the ideas expressed in a piece of writing. Praise your child for this work, explaining exactly what skills were used in this activity.

Revising and Editing Checklist		
Focus/Ideas	Does the report have a clear topic?	
	Does the report stay on topic?	
	Does the report have the right approach for the audience who will read it?	
Organization	Are the ideas presented in a way that makes sense?	
	Are ideas supported by reasons and evidence?	
Conventions	Have you used correct grammar, such as the appropriate verb tense and subject-verb agreement and correct pronoun usage?	
	Is the first word of each sentence capitalized? Are proper nouns (names of people and places) capitalized?	
	Is there a period at the end of each sentence? Are commas, quotation marks, question marks, and other punctuation marks used correctly?	
	Are all words spelled correctly?	

 **Quiz**

Ask your child to revise and edit the following paragraph by writing it correctly in the space provided.

A babysitter must be responsible too many people decide to earn money babysitting without thinking about what it takes to be a good babysitter. First, a babysitter must be careful that young children dont get into a dangerous situation. Young children requires constant attention. Second, a babysitter must be respectful of the familys property. Four example, raiding the refrigerator or scattering belongings in someone else's home is selfish. Third, a babysitter must be nice to the children! Playng with the children and reading books makes these feel liked and well-cared for. Even if their are rules that must be enforced, a babysiter must doing it with kindness.

_____

_____

_____

_____

_____

_____

_____

_____

✓ **Answers**

Note that certain revision changes, such as the concluding sentence, will vary from person to person. Corrected paragraph:

A babysitter must be responsible. Too many people decide to earn money babysitting without thinking about what it takes to be a good babysitter. First, a babysitter must be careful that young children don't get into a dangerous situation. For this reason, young children require constant attention. Second, a babysitter must be respectful of the family's property. For example, raiding the refrigerator or scattering belongings in someone else's home is selfish. Third, a babysitter must be nice to the children! Playing with the children and reading books makes them feel liked and well-cared for. Even if there are rules that must be enforced, a babysitter must do it with kindness. In conclusion, it takes more than just a desire for money to become a babysitter. It also takes responsibility.

OVERVIEW

For Grade 6, the Mathematics Common Core Standards focus heavily on three skill areas. The first skill area focuses on understanding ratios and rates between two quantities, and using ratios and rates to solve real-world and mathematical problems. The second skill area focuses on dividing fractions and graphing on a coordinate plane. The third skill area focuses on using variables to solve basic equations.

Listed below are the Mathematics Common Core Standards for Grade 6 that we have identified as "power standards." We consider these standards to be critical for your child's success. Each lesson in this section focuses on a single standard (or set of related standards) so that you and your child may practice that specific skill to achieve mastery. The applicable standards are divided into three categories: Ratios & Proportional Relationships; The Number System; and Expressions & Equations.

Ratios & Proportional Relationships

1. Basic Ratios with Tables and Tape Diagrams

CCSS.Math.Content.6.RP.A.1: Understand the concept of a ratio and use ratio language to describe a ratio relationship between two quantities. For example, "The ratio of wings to beaks in the bird house at the zoo was 2:1, because for every 2 wings there was 1 beak." "For every vote candidate A received, candidate C received nearly three votes."

CCSS.Math.Content.6.RP.A.3: Use ratio and rate reasoning to solve real-world and mathematical problems, e.g., by reasoning about tables of equivalent ratios or tape diagrams.

CCSS.Math.Content.6.RP.A.3a: Make tables of equivalent ratios relating quantities with whole-number measurements, and find missing values in the tables.

2. Unit Rates and Double Number Line Diagrams

CCSS.Math.Content.6.RP.A.2: Understand the concept of a unit rate $\frac{a}{b}$ associated with a ratio $a{:}b$ with $b \neq 0$, and use rate language in the context of a ratio relationship. For example, "This recipe has a ratio of 3 cups of flour to 4 cups of sugar, so there is $\frac{3}{4}$ cup of flour for each cup of sugar." "We paid $75 for 15 hamburgers, which is a rate of $5 per hamburger."1

CCSS.Math.Content.6.RP.A.3: Use ratio and rate reasoning to solve real-world and mathematical problems, e.g., by reasoning about tables of equivalent ratios or double number line diagrams.

CCSS.Math.Content.6.RP.A.3a: Make tables of equivalent ratios relating quantities with whole-number measurements, and find missing values in the tables.

3. Scaling

CCSS.Math.Content.6.RP.A.3: Use ratio and rate reasoning to solve real-world and mathematical problems, e.g., by reasoning about tables of equivalent ratios, tape diagrams, double number line diagrams, or equations.

CCSS.Math.Content.6.RP.A.3a: Make tables of equivalent ratios relating quantities with whole-number measurements, find missing values in the tables, and plot the pairs of values on the coordinate plane. Use tables to compare ratios.

CCSS.Math.Content.6.RP.A.3b: Solve unit rate problems including those involving unit pricing and constant speed. For example, if it took 7 hours to mow 4 lawns, then at that rate, how many lawns could be mowed in 35 hours? At what rate were lawns being mowed?

CCSS.Math.Content.6.RP.A.3c: Find a percent of a quantity as a rate per 100 (e.g., 30% of a quantity means $\frac{30}{100}$ times the quantity); solve problems involving finding the whole, given a part and the percent.

CCSS.Math.Content.6.RP.A.3d: Use ratio reasoning to convert measurement units; manipulate and transform units appropriately when multiplying or dividing quantities.

4. Percents

CCSS.Math.Content.6.RP.A.3c: Find a percent of a quantity as a rate per 100 (e.g., 30% of a quantity means $\frac{30}{100}$ times the quantity); solve problems involving finding the whole, given a part and the percent.

The Number System

5. Dividing Fractions

CCSS.Math.Content.6.NS.A.1: Interpret and compute quotients of fractions, and solve word problems involving division of fractions by fractions, e.g., by using visual fraction models and equations to represent the problem. For example, create a story context for $\left(\frac{2}{3}\right) \div \left(\frac{3}{4}\right)$ and use a visual fraction model to show the quotient; use the relationship between multiplication and division to explain that $\left(\frac{2}{3}\right) \div \left(\frac{3}{4}\right) = \frac{8}{9}$ because $\frac{3}{4}$ of $\frac{8}{9}$ is $\frac{2}{3}$. (In general, $\left(\frac{a}{b}\right) \div \left(\frac{c}{d}\right) = \frac{ad}{bc}$.) How much chocolate will each person get if 3 people share $\frac{1}{2}$ lb of chocolate equally? How many $\frac{3}{4}$-cup servings are in $\frac{2}{3}$ of a cup of yogurt? How wide is a rectangular strip of land with length $\frac{3}{4}$ mi and area $\frac{1}{2}$ square mi?.

6. Graphing on the Coordinate Plane

CCSS.Math.Content.6.NS.C.8: Solve real-world and mathematical problems by graphing points in all four quadrants of the coordinate plane. Include use of coordinates and absolute value to find distances between points with the same first coordinate or the same second coordinate.

CCSS.Math.Content.6.RP.A.3a: Make tables of equivalent ratios relating quantities with whole-number measurements, find missing values in the tables, and plot the pairs of values on the coordinate plane. Use tables to compare ratios.

Expressions & Equations

7. Equivalent Expressions

CCSS.Math.Content.6.EE.A.3: Apply the properties of operations to generate equivalent expressions. For example, apply the distributive property to the expression $3(2 + x)$ to produce the equivalent expression $6 + 3x$; apply the distributive property to the expression $24x + 18y$ to produce the equivalent expression $6(4x + 3y)$; apply properties of operations to $y + y + y$ to produce the equivalent expression $3y$.

CCSS.Math.Content.6.EE.A.4: Identify when two expressions are equivalent (i.e., when the two expressions name the same number regardless of which value is substituted into them). For example, the expressions $y + y + y$ and $3y$ are equivalent because they name the same number regardless of which number y stands for.

8. Solving Equations

CCSS.Math.Content.6.EE.B.7: Solve real-world and mathematical problems by writing and solving equations of the form $x + p = q$ and $px = q$ for cases in which p, q and x are all nonnegative rational numbers.

9. Using Equations to Solve Problems

CCSS.Math.Content.6.EE.B.5: Understand solving an equation or inequality as a process of answering a question: which values from a specified set, if any, make the equation true? Use substitution to determine whether a given number in a specified set makes an equation or inequality true.

CCSS.Math.Content.6.EE.B.6: Use variables to represent numbers and write expressions when solving a real-world or mathematical problem; understand that a variable can represent an unknown number, or, depending on the purpose at hand, any number in a specified set.

CCSS.Math.Content.6.EE.B.7: Solve real-world and mathematical problems by writing and solving equations of the form $x + p = q$ and $px = q$ for cases in which p, q and x are all nonnegative rational numbers.

10. Independent and Dependent Variables

CCSS.Math.Content.6.EE.C.9: Use variables to represent two quantities in a real-world problem that change in relationship to one another; write an equation to express one quantity, thought of as the dependent variable, in terms of the other quantity, thought of as the independent variable. Analyze the relationship between the dependent and independent variables using graphs and tables, and relate these to the equation. For example, in a problem involving motion at constant speed, list and graph ordered pairs of distances and times, and write the equation $d = 65t$ to represent the relationship between distance and time.

THE STANDARDS

6.RP.A.1: Understand the concept of a ratio and use ratio language to describe a ratio relationship between two quantities. For example, "The ratio of wings to beaks in the bird house at the zoo was 2:1, because for every 2 wings there was 1 beak." "For every vote candidate A received, candidate C received nearly three votes."

6.RP.A.3: Use ratio and rate reasoning to solve real-world and mathematical problems, e.g., by reasoning about tables of equivalent ratios, tape diagrams, double number line diagrams, or equations.

6.RP.A.3a: Make tables of equivalent ratios relating quantities with whole-number measurements, find missing values in the tables, and plot the pairs of values on the coordinate plane. Use tables to compare ratios.

What does it mean?

These mathematics standards focus on problem solving skills that use comparisons and ratios in real-world problems. Solving these types of problems will involve comparing quantities by using visual representations, like tape diagrams, or by looking for patterns in the columns and rows of tables. These comparisons will help establish relationships between quantities that will be further developed in a later lesson using algebraic equations.

Try this together

To learn the skills needed to master the concepts in these standards, your child needs to first understand what a ratio is. A *ratio* is a relationship that compares the relative size of two amounts. You might see ratios written with a colon (2:5), as a fraction $\left(\frac{2}{5}\right)$, or using words (2 to 5). Ratios can compare parts to parts or parts to wholes. For example, suppose you make a fruit salad using 6 oranges, 3 apples, and 2 pears. The ratio of apples to pears is 3:2. The ratio of apples to all the fruit is 3:11.

Some ratios can be simplified, just like a fraction, to create an equivalent ratio. For example, the ratio of apples to oranges in the fruit salad is 3:6 which can also be written as 1:2 because $\frac{3}{6} = \frac{1}{2}$.

A *rate* is a ratio that compares two amounts that have different units, such as 60 miles in 1 hour, $10 for 4 notebooks, or 6 drinks for every 3 people. To solve problems that involve ratios and rates, encourage your child to read the problem, identify the quantities that are being compared, and write them down. Next, ask them to find the relationship between these two quantities, which should be stated in the problem. This relationship is a ratio (or a rate). The ratio will be a basic pattern that your child can apply repeatedly to solve the problem.

Your child has likely seen ratios and rates before and didn't even know it. For example, suppose you go to the grocery store and kiwis are on sale at 3 for $1.00. Your child could use ratios to answer these questions:

If Sara has $4.00, how many kiwis can she buy?
Conversely, how many dollars must Sara have to buy 12 kiwis?

One way to solve these problems is by using a **tape diagram**. First, identify the quantities. The quantities are the number of kiwis and the number of dollars. Next, identify the relationship between the quantities. The relationship, or ratio, of these quantities is 3:1, which is read 3 to 1. You know this because the problem states that for every 3 kiwis, the cost is $1. Now, draw a picture that represents the ratio. To draw a tape diagram, draw the number of rectangles that represent each part of the ratio: 3 rectangles for the 3 kiwis, 1 rectangle for 1 dollar.

Kiwis ▢▢▢

Dollars ▢

This is the basic pattern. Note that the rectangles are all the same size, because each one represents one part. To solve the first problem, repeat the pattern 4 times because Sara has 4 dollars.

Kiwis ▢▢▢ ▢▢▢ ▢▢▢ ▢▢▢

Dollars ▢   ▢   ▢   ▢

Now, look at the diagram—if Sarah has 4 dollars, she can buy 3 + 3 + 3 + 3 = 12 kiwis. Notice that the tape diagram can be used to answer the converse question as well. To buy 12 kiwis, Sara needs 4 dollars.

Another way to solve the problem is by using a **table and repeated addition**. Start by creating a table with two rows, one for each quantity, and a column that relates the two quantities based on the information given in the problem.

Kiwis	3
Dollars	1

As before, the pattern, or ratio, is 3 kiwis for every 1 dollar. Add new columns to the table using the pattern: for every 3 kiwis that are added, 1 more dollar is added. *Note that you are not adding the same number in both rows; this is a common error that many students make. Instead, add the numbers that represent the parts of the ratio to the cells in the corresponding row.*

	+3	+3	+3	
Kiwis	3	6	9	12
Dollars	1	2	3	4
	+1	+1	+1	

Now, read the answer from the table:

Kiwis	3	6	9	12
Dollars	1	2	3	4

Note that the answer is the same as before, 12 kiwis for 4 dollars. Also note that the table can be used to solve the converse problem as well. To buy 12 kiwis, Sara needs 4 dollars.

Kiwis	3	6	9	12
Dollars	1	2	3	4

You can also use a tape diagram to find a part if you know the ratio of the parts and the whole amount. Suppose in a class of 28 students, the ratio of girls to boys is 5:2. How many of the students in the class are boys?

To solve the problem, your child can draw a tape diagram that shows the parts, in the ratio 5:2.

Girls					

Boys		

There are 7 rectangles (parts) in all, and together they represent 28 students, so each rectangle represents 28 ÷ 7 = 4 students. Adding this information to the diagram will help your child visualize how many of the students in the class are boys.

Girls	4	4	4	4	4

Boys	4	4

There are 4 + 4 = 8 boys in the class. Your child can check their answer by finding the number of girls in the class (4 + 4 + 4 + 4 + 4 = 20) and adding it to the number of boys

(20 + 8 = 28). The total should be the same as the total number of students given in the problem.

Now, let's look at a few sample problems that are similar to what a teacher may ask your child to do in class. As you review these problems, note that the standard is not focused only on getting the right answer. In some problems, your child may be asked to use a specific strategy and show their work, or to explain his or her reasoning through words or pictures to demonstrate an understanding of the concepts. You can find answers to these problems in the "Answers" section, as well as an explanation of how they align to the standard.

As you work through these problems, encourage your child to identify the quantities and the relationship between them, i.e. the ratio. Next, have them draw a picture or make a table to represent the relationship. Finally, they should use their picture or table to solve the problem.

? Quiz

1. In a box of candy, there are some pieces of black chocolate and some pieces of white chocolate. When sorted, the pieces from one box look like this:

   What is the simplest ratio of pieces of black chocolate to white chocolate in the box?
   A. 2 to 3   B. 3 to 2   C. 2 to 5   D. 3 to 5

2. During baseball season, Richard gets on base twice for every five times he bats. How many times at bat will it take Richard to get on base 6 times? Draw a tape diagram to support your answer.

3. To make grapefruit punch, James uses 2 cups of grapefruit juice for every 3 cups of ginger ale. How many cups of grapefruit juice should he use if he plans to use 12 cups of ginger ale? Use the table to solve the problem.

Cups of grapefruit juice	2				
Cups of ginger ale	3				

4. Cindy runs 2 miles for every 30 minutes. If she keeps the same pace, how long will it take her to run 5 miles? Use the table to solve the problem.

Miles	1	2	3	4	5
Minutes		30			

5. Erin has 50 coins in her piggy bank. All of the coins are either quarters or dimes. If the ratio of quarters to dimes is 7 to 3, how many quarters does she have? Draw a tape diagram to support your answer.

 Answers

1. In a box of candy, there are some pieces of black chocolate and some pieces of white chocolate. When sorted, the pieces from one box look like this:

    What is the simplest ratio of pieces of black chocolate to white chocolate in the box?

    A. 2 to 3   B. 3 to 2   C. 2 to 5   D. 3 to 5

    The correct answer is B. If you look at the diagram, you see that there are several ratios that describe the number of pieces of black chocolate to white chocolate; these ratios include 9 to 6, 6 to 4, and 3 to 2. The simplest ratio is 3 to 2. You can write ratios to compare parts to parts or parts to wholes. In this question, your child must write a part-to-part ratio, in simplest form. The question addresses standard 6.RP.A.1.

2. During baseball season, Richard gets on base twice for every five times he bats. How many times at bat will it take Richard to get on base 6 times? Draw a tape diagram to support your answer.

    The correct answer is 15 times at bat.

    The problem can be solved by drawing a tape diagram like this:

Times on Base	☐☐		☐☐		☐☐
Times at Bat	☐☐☐☐☐		☐☐☐☐☐		☐☐☐☐☐

    This question requires your child to recognize the quantities involved in a ratio and to draw a tape diagram to answer a real-world question using the ratio. The question addresses standard 6.RP.A.3.

3. To make grapefruit punch, James uses 2 cups of grapefruit juice for every 3 cups of ginger ale. How many cups of grapefruit juice should he use if he plans to use 12 cups of ginger ale? Use the table to solve the problem.

Cups of grapefruit juice	2				
Cups of ginger ale	3				

The correct answer is 8 cups of grapefruit juice. The completed table looks like this:

Cups of grapefruit juice	2	4	6	8	10
Cups of ginger ale	3	6	9	12	15

4. Cindy runs 2 mile for every 30 minutes. If she keeps the same pace, how long will it take her to run 5 miles?

Miles	1	2	3	4	5
Minutes		30			

The correct answer is 75 minutes or 1 hour and 15 minutes. The completed table looks like this:

Miles	1	2	3	4	5
Minutes	15	30	45	60	75

Both questions 3 and 4 require your child to solve a ratio problem by creating a table of equivalent ratios. The questions address standards 6.RP.A.3 and 6.RP.A.3a.

5. Erin has 50 coins in her piggy bank. All of the coins are either quarters or dimes. If the ratio of quarters to dimes is 7 to 3, how many quarters does she have? Draw a tape diagram to support your answer.
The correct answer is 35 quarters.
The problem can be solved by drawing a tape diagram that looks like this:

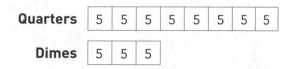

There are 10 parts in all, so each part represents 5 coins, which means she has 7 · 5 = 35 quarters. This question requires your child to draw a tape diagram to find a part given the whole and the ratio in a real-world scenario. The question addresses standard 6.RP.A.3.

THE STANDARDS

6.RP.A.2: *Understand the concept of a unit rate a/b associated with a ratio $\frac{a}{b}$ with b ≠ 0, and use rate language in the context of a ratio relationship. For example, "This recipe has a ratio of 3 cups of flour to 4 cups of sugar, so there is $\frac{3}{4}$ cup of flour for each cup of sugar." "We paid $75 for 15 hamburgers, which is a rate of $5 per hamburger."*

6.RP.A.3: *Use ratio and rate reasoning to solve real-world and mathematical problems, e.g., by reasoning about tables of equivalent ratios, tape diagrams, double number line diagrams, or equations.*

6.RP.A.3a: *Make tables of equivalent ratios relating quantities with whole-number measurements, find missing values in the tables, and plot the pairs of values on the coordinate plane. Use tables to compare ratios.*

What does it mean?

These mathematics standards focus on problem solving skills that involve using unit rates and double number line diagrams to solve real-world problems. In this chapter, the concept of a ratio will be further developed by incorporating new tools and techniques for solving ratio and rate problems.

Try this together

To help your child learn the skills needed to master the concepts in these standards, have them practice reading the problem, identifying the parts of the ratios or rates, and writing the relationship between the parts, which should be stated in the problem. The ratio may be stated in several ways:

- *Quantity 1 to Quantity 2* Example: 4 eggs to 3 cups of flour
- *Quantity 1 for every Quantity 2* Example: 2 teaspoons of cocoa for every 5 ounces of milk
- *Quantity 1: Quantity 2* Example: The ratio of boys to girls in the class is 5:3
- $\frac{Quantity\ 1}{Quantity\ 2}$ *where Quantity 2 is not 0* Example: Lee rode his bike at a rate of

$$\frac{3\ miles}{30\ minutes}$$

- *Quantity 1 per Quantity 2* Example: Mrs. Jones drove at a rate of 60 miles per hour (this is a unit rate because it's 60 miles per 1 hour)

Let's try this problem:

Oranges are on sale at 5 oranges for $1.50. If you have $6.00, how many oranges can you buy?

You could solve this problem using a tape diagram or by making a table of equivalent ratios, like you did in Chapter B, or you could use a **double number line**.

To draw a double number line diagram that represents the problem, first draw two number lines, one to show the number of oranges and one to show the cost. Draw tick marks on each number line that are the same distance apart. Start with zeros for the first tick mark because 0 oranges would cost $0. Then, fill in the rate given in the problem. Because 5 oranges cost $1.50, label them on the same tick mark.

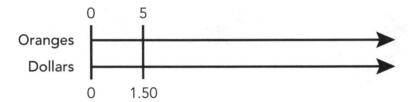

If you buy 5 more oranges, you will have bought 5 1 5 5 10 oranges and the cost will be $1.50 1 $1.50 5 $3.00. These numbers appear on the same tick mark because they are equivalent to the original rate.

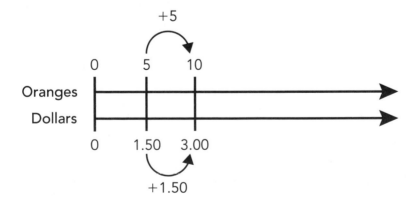

Because the cost of the oranges is a constant rate, each tick mark should increase by the same amount. Keep adding $1.50 to the bottom line until you reach the desired amount, $6.00. Then add 5 oranges at a time to the top line until you reach the last tick mark.

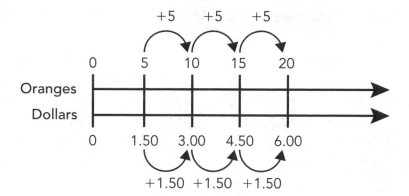

Now, read the number of oranges that corresponds to 6.00: you can buy 20 oranges for $6.00. We solved the problem using a **double number line** and **repeated addition**.

If you need to answer a question that involves much larger numbers, you can use a double number line and **multiplication**, because repeated addition is the same as multiplication. Let's see how!

Suppose you want to buy 45 of the oranges that are on sale. How much will they cost?

Start with the same basic diagram.

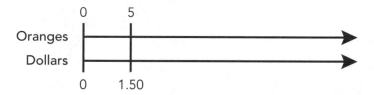

You can find an equivalent rate by multiplying (or dividing) both parts of the rate by the same number. Because you want to buy 45 oranges, and 45 is 9 times 5, multiply both parts of the rate by 9.

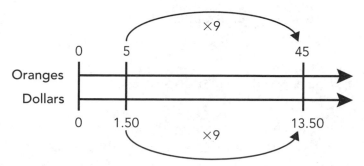

The cost of 45 oranges is $13.50. *Note that both quantities are multiplied by the same number; this preserves the relationship between them.*

Let's solve a similar problem using a table of equivalent ratios.

James can walk 1 mile in 20 minutes. How many miles can he walk in 60 minutes? The quantities being compared are the number of miles James can walk and how many minutes it takes him. The ratio between them is 1 mile to 20 minutes. This type of ratio is called a unit rate; a **unit rate** is a ratio in which one of the numbers is 1. We could solve this problem using a double number line or we could create a table of equivalent ratios. Let's draw a table and fill in what we know.

Miles	1
Minutes	20

To solve the problem, we can use repeated addition or multiplication. The result will be the same.

To use repeated addition, add 1 mile to the amount in each cell in the top row and add 20 minutes to the amount in each cell in the bottom row until you reach 60 minutes. To use multiplication, multiply each cell in both rows by 3, because $20 \times 3 = 60$, which is the desired number of miles.

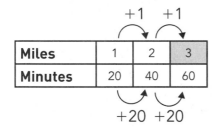 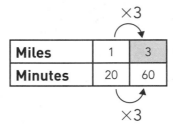

James can walk 3 miles in 60 minutes. *Note that when you use repeated addition, you add each part of the ratio to the corresponding part (row) of the table, but when you use multiplication, you multiply by the same number in both rows.*

In the previous problem, the unit rate was given. Suppose you're given a different rate and need to find the unit rate. Let's try one.

If a train can travel 240 miles in 3 hours, what is the train's rate, or speed, in miles per hour?

In this problem, you are finding a unit rate because *miles per hour* means the number of miles the train can travel in 1 hour. Let's draw a table and fill in **what we know** and **what we need** to solve the problem. Include a column at the beginning of the table for the unit rate. Also include the relationship between the numbers in the row that is completely filled in.

Miles	?	240
Minutes	1	3

To get from 3 hours to 1 hour, you divide by 3. To maintain the same relationship, divide 240 miles by 3 as well.

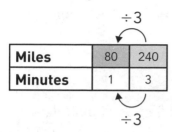

The train's speed is 80 miles per hour.

Now, let's look at a few sample problems. As you work through these problems, encourage your child to identify the quantities and the relationship between them, i.e., the ratio. Also have them practice drawing double number line diagrams or tables to solve the problems.

❓ Quiz

1. To wash his dad's car, Michael needs to combine 0.5 cups of dish detergent for every 5 cups of water. If he has 20 cups of water in his bucket, how many cups of dish detergent does he need? Justify your answer using a double number line diagram.

2. A recipe calls for 3 cups of flour to 2 cups of sugar? How many cups of flour should your use per cup of sugar?

   A. $\frac{2}{3}$ 　　　　 B. 1 　　　　 C. $\frac{3}{2}$ 　　　　 D. 3

3. A box of cereal contains 18 ounces of cereal and costs $3.60. What is the unit price of the cereal, i.e., the price per ounce?
   A. $0.10 　　　 B. $0.20 　　　 C. $1.00 　　　 D. $5.00

4. To make sweet tea, you need 0.75 cups of sugar for every quart of tea. How many cups of sugar will you need to make 6 quarts of sweet tea? Fill in the missing values of the table to answer the question.

Cups of sugar	0.75					
Quarts of tea	1	2	3	4	5	6

5. Kayla is riding her bicycle. It takes her 7 minutes to ride 1 mile. If she maintains an even pace, how long will it take her to ride 9 miles?

    A. 9 minutes   B. 16 minutes   C. 63 minutes   D. 90 minutes

 **Answers**

1. To wash his dad's car, Michael needs to combine 0.5 cups of dish detergent for every 5 cups of water. If he has 20 cups of water in his bucket, how many cups of dish detergent does he need? Justify your answer using a double number line diagram.

   The correct answer is that Michael will need 2 cups of dish detergent. The double number line diagram should look like this:

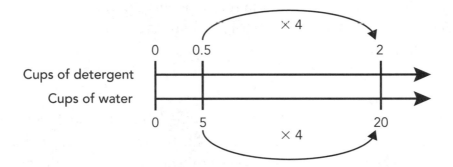

   This question requires your child use ratio and rate reasoning to solve a real-world problem using a double number line diagram. The question addresses standard 6.RP.A.3.

2. A recipe calls for 3 cups of flour to 2 cups of sugar? How many cups of flour should your use per cup of sugar?

   A. $\dfrac{2}{3}$ B. 1   C. $\dfrac{3}{2}$ D. 3

   The correct answer is C. The number of cups of flour per cup of sugar is a unit rate. To determine how much flour is needed for just 1 cup of sugar, divide both parts of the rate by 2 to get $\dfrac{3}{2}$ cups of flour for each $\dfrac{2}{2} = 1$ cup of sugar. You could also draw a table to solve the problem.

3. A box of cereal contains 18 ounces of cereal and costs $3.60. Which is the unit price of the cereal, i.e. the price per ounce?

       A. $0.10   B. $0.20   C. $1.00   D. $5.00

The correct answer is B. You could solve the problem using a table of equivalent ratios, like this:

Dollars	3.60	0.20 (3.60 ÷ 18)
Ounces	18	1 (18 ÷ 18)

Both questions 2 and 3 require your child to find a unit rate by interpreting information given in a word problem. The questions address standard 6.RP.A.2.

4. To make sweet tea, you need 0.75 cups of sugar for every quart of tea. How many cups of sugar will you need to make 6 quarts of sweet tea? Fill in the missing values of the table to answer the question.

   The correct answer is 4.5 cups of sugar. Below is the table with the missing values filled in. To complete the top row, 0.75 was added to the amount in the previous cell to create equivalent ratios. The process was repeated until 6 quarts of tea was reached.

Cups of sugar	0.75	1.5	2.25	3	3.75	4.5
Quarts of tea	1	2	3	4	5	6

This question requires your child to use ratio and rate reasoning to solve a real-world problem using a table of equivalent ratios. The question addresses standards 6.RP.A.3 and 6.RP.A.3a.

5. Kayla is riding her bicycle. It takes her 7 minutes to ride 1 mile. If she maintains an even pace, how long will it take her to ride 9 miles?

   A. 9 minutes   B. 16 minutes   C. 63 minutes   D. 90 minutes

   The correct answer is C. The unit rate is given in the problem: 1 mile to 7 minutes. You can use multiplication and a table or a double number line diagram to find that she bikes 1 × 9 = 9 miles in 7 × 9 = 63 minutes.

   This question involves using a unit rate to solve a real-world problem. The question addresses standards 6.RP.A.2 and 6.RP.A.3.

THE STANDARDS

6.RP.A.3: Use ratio and rate reasoning to solve real-world and mathematical problems, e.g., by reasoning about tables of equivalent ratios, tape diagrams, double number line diagrams, or equations.

6.RP.A.3a: Make tables of equivalent ratios relating quantities with whole-number measurements, find missing values in the tables, and plot the pairs of values on the coordinate plane. Use tables to compare ratios.

6.RP.A.3b: Solve unit rate problems including those involving unit pricing and constant speed. For example, if it took 7 hours to mow 4 lawns, then at that rate, how many lawns could be mowed in 35 hours? At what rate were lawns being mowed?

6.RP.A.3d: Use ratio reasoning to convert measurement units; manipulate and transform units appropriately when multiplying or dividing quantities.

What does it mean?

These mathematics standards focus on the problem solving skills that your child learned in previous lessons. These skills will be further developed to include scaling a rate up or down, and will be applied to new types of real-world problems that involve unit conversions and scale models.

Encourage your child to use a consistent strategy for solving the problems. The strategy should include these steps:

1. Identify the quantities that are related and write them down.
2. Find the relationship between these quantities, which should be stated in the problem, and express the relationship as a ratio (or a rate).
3. Use an appropriate tool, such as a tape diagram, double number line, or table of equivalent ratios to solve the problem.

Try this together

In the previous lesson, your child learned to use a unit rate to find equivalent rates that involved larger numbers, through multiplication. In this lesson, your child will learn to **scale down** a rate, through division, to find the equivalent unit rate, and then apply a technique called **scaling down to scale up**, which is helpful when the numbers in the problem aren't multiples of each other.

Suppose you want to buy 12 oranges that are on sale at 5 oranges for $1.50. How much will they cost?

This time, let's start with a diagram similar to the one we used in the previous lesson, but leave a little room to work.

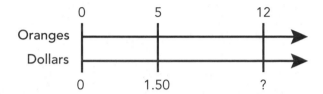

You want to buy 12 oranges, but there is no easy number to multiply 5 by to get 12. Instead, you can **scale down** to find the unit price (the cost of 1 orange) by dividing both parts of the given rate by 5.

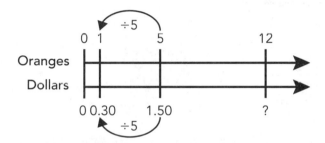

The cost is 30¢ for 1 orange. Now, you can **scale up** the unit price to 12 oranges by multiplying both parts of the unit price by 12.

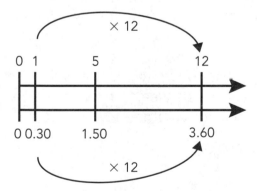

The cost of 12 oranges is $3.60.

Let's try another example of scaling down to scale up using a table of equivalent ratios: Suppose Margo walks 2 miles in 42 minutes. If she continues to walk at that speed, how long will it take her to walk 3 miles?

Just like in the previous example, 3 miles and 2 miles don't divide evenly, so we need to scale down the give rate to find the unit rate, and then scale up the unit rate to the desired number of miles. Let's start by drawing a table and filling in what we know and what we need to find. Include a row for the unit rate.

Miles	Minutes
1	?
2	42
3	?

To get from 2 miles to 1 mile, divide both parts of the given rate by 2. Then, to get from 1 mile to 3 miles, multiply both parts of the unit rate by 3.

Miles	Minutes
1 (2 ÷ 2)	21 (42 ÷ 2)
2	42
3	?

→

Miles	Minutes
1	21
2	42
3 (1 × 3)	63 (21 × 3)

It will take Margo about 63 minutes to walk 3 miles.

Other types of problem that can be solved using unit rates are **scale models** and **unit conversions**.

Suppose Cho looks on a map and finds a scale that says 1 inch equals 100 miles. He measures the distance on the map between two cities and finds that they are 6 inches apart. How far apart are the two cities?

Let's start by drawing a table. The scale says that 1 inch equals 100 miles, so put those values in the same column of the table. The distance between the two cities on the map is 6 inches, so place that value in the table in the inches column.

Miles	100	
Inches	1	6

The relationship between the two columns in the bottom row is that 6 inches is 1 inch multiplied by 6. So, multiply the 100 miles in the top row by 6 to get the answer:

Miles	100	600 (100 × 6)
Inches	1	6 (1 × 6)

The two cities are 600 miles apart.

Students often have trouble remembering whether to multiply or divide when **converting between units**. Using a table may help your child avoid this common problem. Let's see how.

There are 32 fluid ounces in 1 quart. How many fluid ounces are in 4 quarts?

Draw a table and include what you know and what you need to find. Then look for the relationship between the columns and apply the same operation to the missing amount.

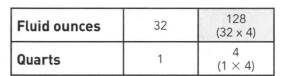

Fluid ounces	32	?
Quarts	1	4 (1 × 4)

→

Fluid ounces	32	128 (32 x 4)
Quarts	1	4 (1 × 4)

There are 128 fluid ounces in 4 quarts.

Now, let's try some practice problems. As your child works through the problems, encourage them to use the steps presented at the beginning of the lesson and to use a double number line diagram or a table to help them solve the problems.

Quiz

1. Julio can build 3 birdhouses in 6 hours. How long does it take Julio to build 5 birdhouses?

   A. 2 hours   *B. 3 hours*   *C. 9 hours*   *D. 10 hours*

2. The Martins are taking a vacation. Before lunch they travel 260 miles in 4 hours. If they travel at the same average rate after lunch, how long will it take them to drive 390 more miles? Justify your answer using a double number line diagram.

3. The key on a map says 1 cm = 75 miles. The distance from New York City to Washington, D.C. is about 225 miles. How far apart are New York City and Washington, D.C. on this map?

   A. 2 cm   *B. 2.5 cm*   *C. 3 cm*   *D. 3.5 cm*

4. James is 48 inches tall. If 1 inch equals about 2.5 centimeters, what is James's approximate height in centimeters? Justify your answer using a table.

5. The veterinarian weighs Susan's dog at 8.0 kilograms. There are 2.2 pounds for every kilogram. How many pounds does Susan's dog weigh?

Answers

1. Julio can build 3 birdhouses in 6 hours. How long does it take Julio to build 5 bird-houses?

   A. 2 hours   *B. 3 hours*   *C. 9 hours*   *D. 10 hours*

   The correct answer is D. Scale down the given rate to find the unit rate, or how long it takes Julio to build 1 birdhouse, by dividing both parts of the rate by 3. The unit rate is 2 hours for every 1 birdhouse. Then scale up the unit rate to 5 birdhouses by multiplying both parts of the rate by 5. It takes Julio 2 × 5 = 10 hours to build 5 birdhouses.

   This question requires your child to use ratio and rate reasoning to solve a real-world problem. The question addresses standard 6.RP.A.3.

2. The Martins are taking a vacation. Before lunch they travel 260 miles in 4 hours. If they travel at the same average rate after lunch, how long will it take them to drive 390 more miles? Justify your answer using a double number line diagram.

   The correct answer is 6 hours. Here's what your double number line diagram might look like:

   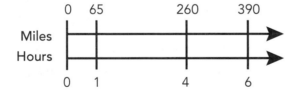

   This question requires your child to find a unit rate that represents a constant speed and then solve a problem using the unit rate. The question addresses standards 6.RP.A.3 and 6.RP.A.3b.

3. The key on a map says 1 cm = 75 miles. The distance from New York City to Washington, D.C. is about 225 miles. How far apart are New York City and Washington, D.C. on this map?

   A. 2 cm   *B. 2.5 cm*   *C. 3 cm*   *D. 3.5 cm*

   The correct answer is C. If you solved the problem using a table, here's what it might look like:

Centimeters	1	3 (1 × 3)
Miles	75	225 (75 × 3)

   This question requires your child to use ratio and rate reasoning to solve a real-world problem. The problem addresses standard 6.RP.A.3.

4. James is 48 inches tall. If 1 inch equals about 2.5 centimeters, what is James's approximate height in centimeters? Justify your answer using a table.

    The correct answer is that James is approximately 120 centimeters tall. The table might look like this:

Inches	1	48 (1 × 48)
Centimeters	2.5	120 (2.5 × 48)

5. The veterinarian weighs Susan's dog at 8.0 kilograms. There are 2.2 pounds for every kilogram. How many pounds does Susan's dog weigh?

    The correct answer is that Susan's dog weighs 17.6 pounds. If you solved the problem using a table, here's what it might look like:

Pounds	2.2	17.6 (2.2 × 8)
Kilograms	1	8 (1 × 8)

Questions 4 and 5 require your child to use tables of equivalent ratios to solve real world problems involving unit conversions. The questions address standards 6.RP.A.3a and 6.RP.A.3d.

THE STANDARD

6.RP.A.3c: *Find a percent of a quantity as a rate per 100 (e.g., 30% of a quantity means 30/100 times the quantity); solve problems involving finding the whole, given a part and the percent.*

What does it mean?

This mathematics standard focuses on using ratios to solve real-world problems that involve percents. This is an extension of the problem solving skills that your child learned in previous lessons.

Try this together

Stress to your child that a **percent** is simply a rate for each hundred. The word *per* means *for each*, and the word *cent* means *hundred*. Twenty percent means 20 for each 100, so it can be written as the ratio $\frac{20}{100}$. Because it is a ratio, you can solve percent problems using the same techniques as before, such as by using a double number line diagram.

There are three types of percent problems that your child might encounter.

1. Find a percent of a whole amount, which equals a part of that amount.
2. Find a percent when given a part and a whole amount.
3. Find the whole amount when given a part and the percent of the whole that that part represents.

A good example of the first type of problem is sales tax. Suppose the sales tax in a state is 7%. Dana wants to buy an item that costs $30. How much sales tax will she have to pay?

Here's how to solve the problem using a double number line diagram.

Draw and label a double number line by putting 0s on the first tick mark and the tax rate on another tick mark. Remember that 7% means 7 dollars in tax for every 100 dollars that an item costs. Dana is buying a $30 item, which is less than $100, so place the tick mark relating 7 dollars and 100 dollars further away from the 0-0 line. Then label a tick mark to represent what you're looking for.

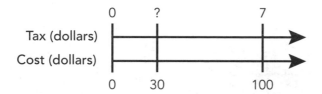

Now, how does 30 dollars relate to 100 dollars? In other words, what do you have to multiply 100 by to get 30? If you said 0.3, then you are correct. To find an equivalent ratio, multiply 7 by 0.3 as well, like this:

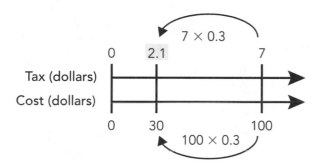

This means Dana must pay $2.10 in sales tax when she buys a $30 item. Note that some questions may ask for the total cost of the item, in which case you must add the sales tax to the original cost. In this example, Dana's total cost, including sales tax, would be $30 + $2.10 = $32.10.

Now let's try an example of the second type of problem. To make cran-apple juice, David adds 2 cups of cranberry juice to 3 cups of apple juice. What is the percentage of cranberry juice in the mixture? Note that the total volume of the mixture is 5 cups (2 cups of cranberry juice + 3 cups of apple juice).

Let's draw a double number line diagram that shows what we know and what we need to find. Remember, *percent* means *per hundred*. We know that in a mixture with 5 cups of juice, 2 cups are cranberry juice. How many cups of cranberry juice would we need to make 100 cups of the mixture?

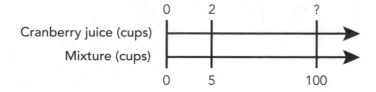

How does 100 cups relate to 5 cups? We know that 5 times 20 is 100, so to keep the same ratio, we need to multiply 2 times 20 as well.

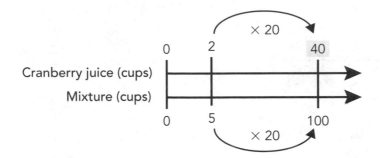

There would be 40 cups of cranberry juice in 100 cups of the mixture, which represents a ratio of $\frac{40}{100}$ or 40%.

Finally, let's look at the third type of percent problem: finding the whole amount when you know a part and the percent that that part represents.

Rochelle needs to read 3 chapters in her novel over the weekend. So far, she has read 9 pages, which represents 45% of all the pages she needs to read. How many pages are in the 3 chapters?

To solve the problem, start by drawing a double number line that includes tick marks for what you know and what you need to find. Remember, 45% means 45 out of 100. Because 9 is less than 45, draw the tick mark for 9 pages between 0 and 45.

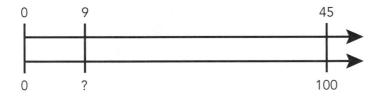

Looking at the top line, we know that 9 is 45 ÷ 5, so we need to divide 100 by 5 to keep the same ratio.

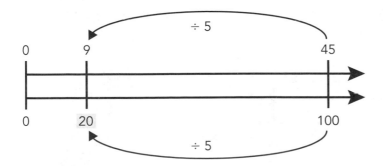

There are 20 pages in the 3 chapters that Rochelle needs to read.

Now it's time to practice solving some percent problems.

 Quiz

1. What is 40% of 15? Draw a double number line diagram to support your answer.

2. In a lab experiment, John adds 40 milliliters of vegetable oil to a beaker containing 160 milliliters of water. What percentage of the mixture in the beaker is vegetable oil?
   A. 10%   B. 20%   C. 25%   D. 40%

3. Janet paid $530 for a $500 television. What was the sale tax rate as a percentage?
   A. 3%   B. 6%   C. 18%   D. 30%

4. Roberta must pay a 20% fee for making her loan payment late. If the payment is normally $150.00, how much is her late fee?

5. The percentage of sugar in a canned drink is 25% by weight. If the weight of the sugar is 6 ounces, how many ounces are in the drink altogether?

 **Answers**

Questions 1–5 require your child to solve problems involving percents. Some of the questions require finding a percent of a number, some require finding a part of a number given the percent, and some require finding the whole amount when given a part and the percent. Each question assesses your child's understanding that a percent is a rate per 100. The questions address the standard 6.RP.A.3c.

1. What is 40% of 15? Draw a double number line diagram to support your answer.

   The correct answer is 6. Here is the solution shown on a double number line:

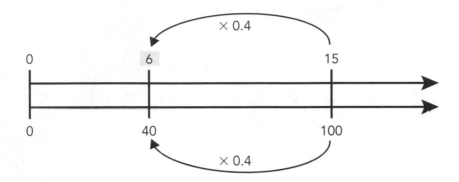

2. In a lab experiment, John adds 40 milliliters of vegetable oil to a beaker containing 160 milliliters of water. What percentage of the mixture in the beaker is vegetable oil?

   A. 10%   *B. 20%*   *C. 25%*   *D. 40%*

   The correct answer is B. To solve the problem, note that the total amount of liquid in the beaker is 40 + 160 = 200 milliliters. You could draw a double number line like this:

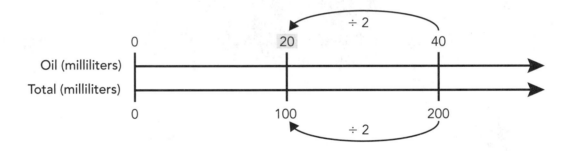

3. Janet paid $530 for a $500 television. What was the sale tax rate as a percentage?

   A. 3%   *B. 6%*   *C. 18%*   *D. 30%*

   The correct answer is B. Janet paid $30 in tax on the $500 television ($530 −$500 = $30), so you are trying to find what percent of 500 is 30. Here's a double number line diagram that shows the solution.

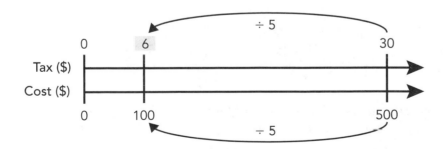

4. Roberta must pay a 20% fee for making her loan payment late. If the payment is normally $150.00, how much is her late fee?

   The correct answer is $30. The late fee is $20 for every $100, so you need to find how many dollars the late fee is for $150. Here's a double number line diagram that shows the solution.

5. The percentage of sugar in a canned drink is 25% by weight. If the weight of the sugar is 6 ounces, how many ounces are in the drink altogether?

   The correct answer is 24 ounces. To make the numbers easier to work with, you can think of 25% as $\dfrac{25}{100}$ which is equivalent to $\dfrac{1}{4}$. Here's a double number line diagram that shows the solution.

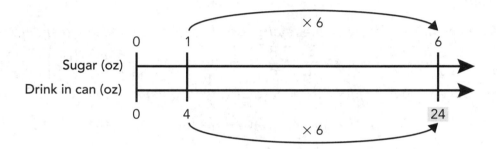

THE STANDARD

6.NS.A.1: Interpret and compute quotients of fractions, and solve word problems involving division of fractions by fractions, e.g., by using visual fraction models and equations to represent the problem. For example, create a story context for $\left(\frac{2}{3}\right) \div \left(\frac{3}{4}\right)$ and use a visual fraction model to show the quotient; use the relationship between multiplication and division to explain that $\left(\frac{2}{3}\right) \div \left(\frac{3}{4}\right) = \frac{8}{9}$ because $\frac{3}{4}$ of $\frac{8}{9}$ is $\frac{2}{3}$. (In general, $\left(\frac{a}{b}\right) \div \left(\frac{c}{d}\right) = \frac{ad}{bc}$.) How much chocolate will each person get if 3 people share $\frac{1}{2}$ lb. of chocolate equally? How many $\frac{3}{4}$-cup servings are in $\frac{2}{3}$ of a cup of yogurt? How wide is a rectangular strip of land with length $\frac{3}{4}$ mi and area $\frac{1}{2}$ square mi?

What does it mean?

This mathematics standard focuses on skills needed to solve problems that involve dividing one fraction by another fraction. Solutions may include the use of visual models, an understanding of how multiplication and division are related, or the use of a general formula for dividing fractions.

Try this together

Here's a problem: Jim has $\frac{1}{2}$ of a candy bar. He wants to divide the candy bar amongst his friends, giving each friends $\frac{1}{4}$ candy bar. How many friends can he give candy to? In order words, how many groups of $\frac{1}{4}$ can he make out of $\frac{1}{2}$, or what is $\frac{1}{2} \div \frac{1}{4}$?

This problem can be solved visually or numerically. First, let's use a visual model to solve the problem:

Draw a rectangle to represent a whole candy bar.

Divide the rectangle into 2 equal pieces and shade one of them to show the amount that Jim has, one half of a candy bar.

Below the rectangle, draw a second rectangle that is the same size. Divide this rectangle into 4 equal pieces to show fourths.

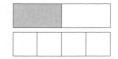

Now, shade in the number of $\frac{1}{4}$ pieces that equal $\frac{1}{2}$ the candy bar. Count how many pieces are shaded.

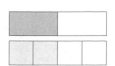

There are two $\frac{1}{4}$ pieces that are shaded, so there are 2 groups of $\frac{1}{4}$ that will fit into $\frac{1}{2}$. Jim can give candy to 2 of his friends.

$$\frac{1}{2} \div \frac{1}{4} = 2$$

Another way to solve the problem is by finding a common denominator and using what you know about multiplication. That is, when you multiply two fractions, you can simply multiply the numerators and multiply the denominators. When dividing fractions, this becomes quite easy when the fractions have the same denominator. Let's see.

Our problem is $\frac{1}{2} \div \frac{1}{4} = ?$ We can write $\frac{1}{2}$ with a denominator of 4 like this: $\frac{1}{2} \times \frac{2}{2} = \frac{2}{4}$. So the problem can be rewritten as $\frac{2}{4} \div \frac{1}{4} = ?$ Now, just like with multiplication, you can divide the numerators and divide the denominators, like this: $\frac{2}{4} \div \frac{1}{4} = \frac{2 \div 1}{4 \div 4} = \frac{2}{1}$, or just 2. The quotient is the same as before.

Finally, the problem can be solved using this general formula for dividing fractions:

$$\frac{a}{b} \div \frac{c}{d} = \frac{a}{b} \times \frac{d}{c} = \frac{ad}{bc}$$

In words, this formula says that to divide one fraction by another fraction, you multiply the first fraction by the reciprocal (flip it) of the second fraction. Let's try it out on our problem.

$$\frac{1}{2} \div \frac{1}{4} = \frac{1}{2} \times \frac{4}{1} = \frac{4}{2} = 2$$

The formula works! The quotient is the same as before.

Now, let's work a few problems. Don't forget, you can find answers to these problems in the "Answers" section, as well as an explanation of how they align to the standard.

? Quiz

1. Karen is cooking rice. The directions on the box say to use $\frac{3}{4}$ cups of rice and 1 cup of water to make one serving. Karen measures the rice left in the box and finds that there are 3 cups of rice. How many servings can Karen make? Draw a model to support your answer.

2. Which expression shows a strategy for dividing $\frac{2}{5}$ by $\frac{1}{25}$?

   A. $\frac{2 \cdot 1}{5 \cdot 25}$ B. $\frac{2 \cdot 25}{5 \cdot 1}$ C. $\frac{5 \cdot 1}{2 \cdot 25}$ D. $\frac{5 \cdot 25}{2 \cdot 1}$

3. A rectangular parking lot at a shopping mall has an area of $\frac{1}{32}$ square mile. If the width of the parking lot is $\frac{1}{8}$ mile, how long is the parking lot?

4. How many $\frac{1}{6}$ portions of a candy bar can you get out of $\frac{2}{3}$ of a candy bar? Draw a model to support your answer.

5. If you have $3\frac{3}{4}$ pounds of ground meat and each hamburger contains $\frac{3}{8}$ pounds, how many hamburgers can you make?

Answers

1. Karen is cooking rice. The directions on the box say to use $\frac{3}{4}$ cups of rice and 1 cup of water to make one serving. Karen measures the rice left in the box and finds that there are 3 cups of rice. How many servings can Karen make? Draw a model to support your answer.

The correct answer is 4 servings. In the diagram below, the 3 cups of rice are represented by 3 rectangles. Below them are the same rectangles, divided into fourths. Three-fourths at a time are shaded to represent $\frac{3}{4}$ cups. There are 4 sets of three shaded portions, which means that Karen can make 4 servings of rice.

1 cup	1 cup	1 cup

Questions 1 – 5 address various parts of standard 6.NS.A.1. This question requires your child to visually solve a problem that involves dividing a fraction by another fraction.

2. Which expression shows a strategy for dividing $\frac{2}{5}$ by $\frac{1}{25}$?

A. $\frac{2 \cdot 1}{5 \cdot 25}$ B. $\frac{2 \cdot 25}{5 \cdot 1}$ C. $\frac{5 \cdot 1}{2 \cdot 25}$ D. $\frac{5 \cdot 25}{2 \cdot 1}$

The correct answer is B. To divide by $\frac{1}{25}$, multiply by its reciprocal, $\frac{25}{1}$. Then you can multiply the numerators and multiply the denominators.

$$\frac{2}{5} \div \frac{1}{25} = \frac{2}{5} \cdot \frac{25}{1} = \frac{2 \cdot 25}{5 \cdot 1}$$

This question assesses your child's understanding of how to apply the general formula for dividing a fraction by another fraction.

3. A rectangular parking lot at a shopping mall has an area of $\frac{1}{32}$ square mile. If the width of the parking lot is $\frac{1}{8}$ mile, how long is the parking lot?

The correct answer is $\frac{1}{4}$ mile. You can find the area of a rectangle by multiplying the length times the width, $A = l \cdot w$. If you know the area, you can find one of the dimensions by dividing the area by the other dimension. Here, you know the area and the width, so divide to find the length:

$$\frac{1}{32} \div \frac{1}{8} = \frac{1}{32} \cdot \frac{8}{1} = \frac{8}{32} = \frac{1}{4}$$

This question requires your child to solve a word problem involving division of a fraction by another fraction.

4. How many $\frac{1}{6}$ portions of a candy bar can you get out of $\frac{2}{3}$ of a candy bar? Draw a model to support your answer.

The correct answer is 4. Your model might look like this:

This question requires your child to visually solve a problem that involves dividing a fraction by another fraction.

5. If you have $3\frac{3}{4}$ pounds of ground meat and each hamburger contains $\frac{3}{8}$ pounds, how many hamburgers can you make?

The correct answer is 10 hamburgers. First, write the mixed number as a fraction.

$$3\frac{3}{4} \div \frac{3}{8} = \frac{15}{4} \div \frac{3}{8}$$

Then use common denominators or the general formula for dividing fractions. If you use common denominators, the solution looks like this:

$$\frac{15}{4} \div \frac{3}{8} = \frac{30}{8} \div \frac{3}{8} = \frac{30 \div 3}{8 \div 8} = \frac{10}{1} = 10$$

This question requires your child to solve a word problem involving division of a fraction by another fraction.

THE STANDARDS

6.NS.C.8: *Solve real-world and mathematical problems by graphing points in all four quadrants of the coordinate plane. Include use of coordinates and absolute value to find distances between points with the same first coordinate or the same second coordinate.*

6.RP.A.3a: *Make tables of equivalent ratios relating quantities with whole-number measurements, find missing values in the tables, and plot the pairs of values on the coordinate plane. Use tables to compare ratios.*

What does it mean?

These mathematics standards focus on graphing on a coordinate plane. Students will learn how to plot points on a coordinate plane and to find the distance between two points when they share a common horizontal or vertical coordinate. Students will also learn how to solve ratio problems by graphing points on a coordinate plane. Graphing skills are essential for higher mathematics, like algebra and geometry, and for other subjects such as science and business.

Try this together

On a sheet of paper or graph paper, practice drawing and labeling a standard coordinate plane, like the one below. Notice that the horizontal axis is labeled *x* and the vertical axis is labeled *y*. The point where the axes cross is called the **origin**. The origin has the coordinates (0, 0). The two axes form a plane and divide the plane into four quadrants.

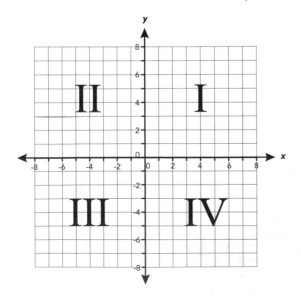

1. Quadrant I is the upper right quadrant. The points in this quadrant have coordinates (*x, y*) because they are to the right of and above the origin. Both coordinates are positive numbers.
2. Quadrant II is the upper left quadrant. The points in this quadrant have coordinates (*–x, y*) because they are to the left of, but still above, the origin.
3. Quadrant III is the lower left quadrant. The points in this quadrant have coordinates (*–x, –y*) because they are to the left of and below the origin. Both coordinates are negative numbers.
4. Quadrant IV is the lower right quadrant. The points in this quadrant have coordinates (*x, –y*) because they are to the right of, but below, the origin.

To plot points on the coordinate plane, you need an ordered pair of numbers (number 1, number 2). Let's plot the ordered pair (3, 5). The first number is the *x*-coordinate, which represents horizontal movement. The second number is the *y*-coordinate, which represents vertical movement. To plot the point, notice that both coordinates are positive numbers. This means that you should move to the right and up. Start at the origin and move to the right (along the *x*-axis) 3 units. Keep your pencil where it is (at *x* = 3) and move up 5 units. Draw a point and label it *A*. Next to the label, write the coordinates of the point, (3, 5).

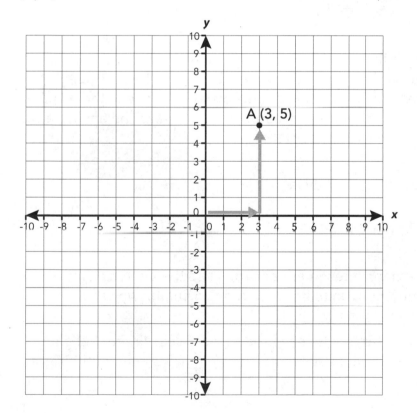

Now, let's plot a second point on the coordinate plane with the coordinates (–3, 5) and label it *B*. Just remember to move in alphabetical order, horizontal then vertical. Start at the origin and move left 3 units, then up 5 units.

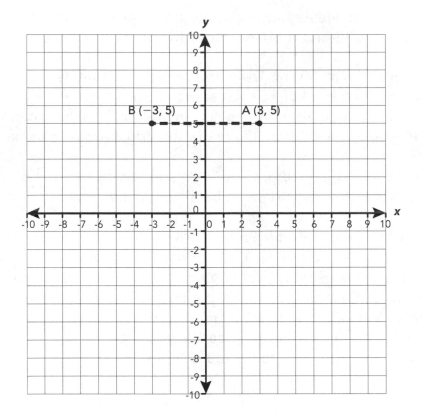

Now, suppose we want to find the distance between the two points. We can show this distance by drawing a dotted line connecting *A* and *B*. Notice that the points have the same *y*-coordinate (5). This means that we can find the distance between the points by taking the absolute value of the difference in the *x*-coordinates. (We take the absolute value because distance can't be a negative amount.) Let's see.

The distance between (3, 5) and (–3, 5) is:

$$|3 - (-3)| = |3 + 3| = |6| = 6 \text{ OR } |-3 - 3| = |-6| = 6$$

You can subtract the *x*-coordinates in either order and the distance will be the same. You could also count the number of units between the two points, which is 6.

This method also works if two points have the same *x*-coordinate. Let's plot a third point with the coordinates (3, –5) and label it *C*. This time, move 3 units to the right of the origin and down 5 units.

Now, let's find the distance between *A* and *C*. This time, the points have the same *x*-coordinate (3), so the distance between them is the absolute value of the difference in their *y*-coordinates:

$$|5 - (-5)| = |5 + 5| = |10| = 10 \text{ OR } |-5 - 5| = |-10| = 10$$

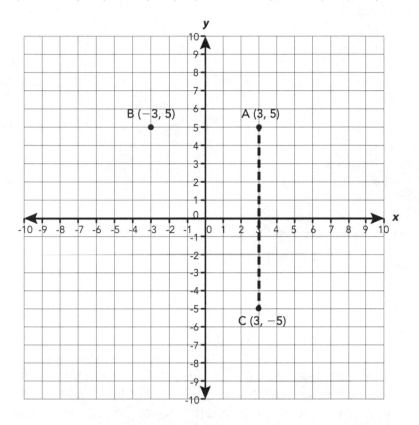

We can also use coordinate planes to solve ratio problems. Here is an example that we saw in a previous lesson: At the grocery store, kiwis are on sale at 3 for $1.00. How much do 12 kiwis cost? Before, we solved the problem using a table and repeated addition, like this:

Kiwis	3	6	9	12
Dollars	1	2	3	4

According to the table, 12 kiwis cost $4. Here's how you can solve the same problem using a coordinate plane.

If you let the horizontal axis represent the number of kiwis you buy and the vertical axis represent how much the kiwis cost, then the ratio 3 kiwis:1 dollar could be represented by the coordinate point (3, 1). To plot more points, follow the repeated addition pattern in the table: + 3 kiwis, + 1 dollar. On the graph, this means to move to the right 3 and up 1 each time. Here's what the graph should look like:

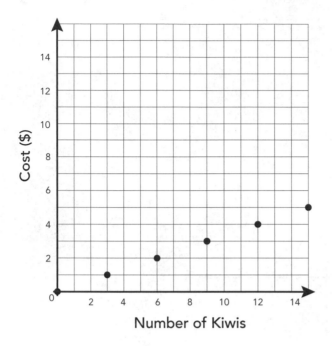

To solve the problem, find 12 on the horizontal axis and read the corresponding value on the vertical axis, which is $4.

Notice that we only drew the first quadrant of the coordinate plane this time. That's because you can't have less than 0 kiwis (no negative values of *x*) and you can't have less than 0 dollars (no negative values of *y*). Real-world problems are often (but not always) restricted to the first quadrant. The situation determines which quadrants you need to include. For example, if you were recording temperatures, you might have negative values because the temperature can drop below 0.

Now, let's practice a few problems that your child may see in class, on homework, or when it's time for a test.

❓ Quiz

Use the graph at right to answer questions 1-2.

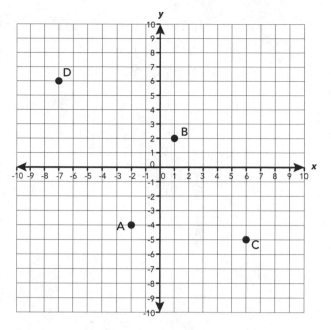

1. Which point on the graph has the coordinates (6, –5)?
    A. point A
    B. point B
    C. point C
    D. point D

2. What are the coordinates of point *D*?
    A. (–4, –2)
    B. (6, –7)
    C. (6, –5)
    D. (–7, 6)

Use the graph below to answer questions 3-4.

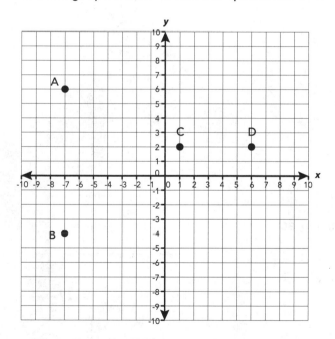

3. What is the distance between points *A* and *B*?

4. What is the distance between points *C* and *D*?

5. To make cheese omelets, Daniel uses 2 cups of cheese for every 3 eggs. If Daniel has 15 eggs, how many cups of cheese should he use? Support your answer using the co-ordinate plane below.

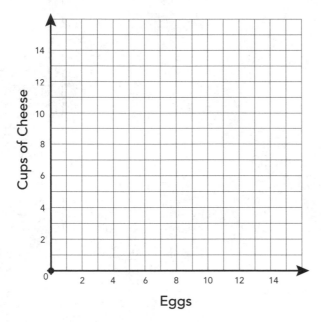

Eggs

 **Answers**

Use the graph at right to answer questions 1-2.

1. Which point on the graph has the co-ordinates (6, –5)?

   A. point A   B. point B

   C. point C   D. point D

   The correct answer is C. Point C has the coordinates (6, –5).

2. What are the coordinates of point D?

   A. (–4, –2)   B. (6, –7)

   C. (6, –5)   D. (–7, 6)

   The correct answer is D. Point D has the coordinates (–7, 6).

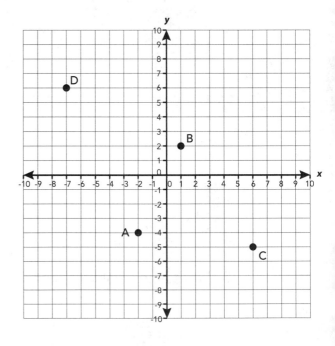

Questions 1 and 2 require your child to be able to plot points on a coordinate plane and to read the coordinates of the points. The questions address standard 6.NS.C.8.

Use the graph at right to answer questions 3-4.

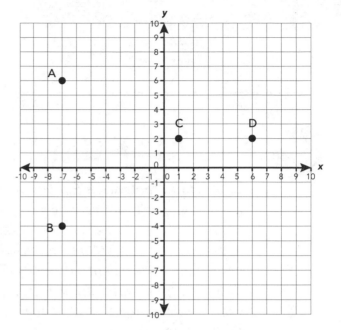

3. What is the distance between points *A* and *B*?

   The correct answer is 10 units. Point A has coordinates (–7, 6) and point B has coordinates (–7, –4). The points have the same x-coordinates, so the distance is the absolute value of the difference in their y-coordinates: $|6 - (-4)| = |6 + 4| = |10| = 10$ or $|-4 - 6| = |-10| = 10$.

4. What is the distance between points *C* and *D*?

   The correct answer is 5 units. Point C has coordinates (1, 2) and point B has coordinates (6, 2). The points have the same y-coordinates, so the distance is the absolute value of the difference in their x-coordinates: $|6 - 1| = |5| = 5$ or $|1 - 6| = |-5| = 5$.

   Questions 3 and 4 require your child to find the distance between two points on a coordinate plane where both points share either an x-coordinate or a y-coordinate. The questions address standard 6.NS.C.8.

5. To make cheese omelets, Daniel uses 2 cups of cheese for every 3 eggs. If Daniel has 15 eggs, how many cups of cheese should he use? Support your answer using the coordinate plane below.

   The correct answer is 10 cups of cheese. Here's what the graph should look like:

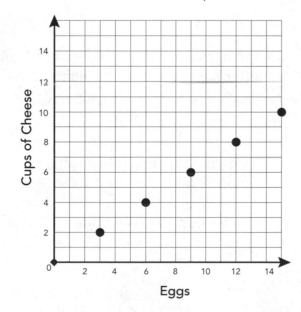

This question requires your child to solve a ratio problem by plotting pairs of values on a coordinate. The question addresses standard 6.RP.A.3a.

THE STANDARDS

CCSS.Math.Content.6.EE.A.3: Apply the properties of operations to generate equivalent expressions. For example, apply the distributive property to the expression 3 (2 + x) to produce the equivalent expression 6 + 3x; apply the distributive property to the expression 24x + 18y to produce the equivalent expression 6 (4x + 3y); apply properties of operations to y + y + y to produce the equivalent expression 3y.

CCSS.Math.Content.6.EE.A.4: Identify when two expressions are equivalent (i.e., when the two expressions name the same number regardless of which value is substituted into them). For example, the expressions y + y + y and 3y are equivalent because they name the same number regardless of which number y stands for.

What does it mean?

These mathematics standards focus on identifying, writing, and evaluating equivalent expressions by using properties of operations, such as the distributive property and the commutative property of addition. Because equations are expressions that are set equal to each other, by developing an understanding of how to work with equivalent expressions, your child is building a foundation for solving equations later.

Try this together

In math, an **expression** is a grouping of numbers, operations $(+, -, \times, \div)$, and at least one unknown, or variable, represented by a letter such as x or y, that shows the value of something. Here is an example of an expression: $x + 2 + 3x + 6$. If x is equal to 5, the value of this expression is $5 + 2 + 3(5) + 6 = 28$.

Two expressions are **equivalent** if they name the same number regardless of what value is substituted into them. To write equivalent expressions, you can apply properties of operations, such as the commutative property of addition or the distributive property. Let's apply the commutative property to our example. The property states that $a + b = b + a$, so we can change the order of the terms in the expression and it will not change its value:

$$x + 2 + 3x + 6 = x + 3x + 2 + 6$$

We can also add like terms together, which is sometimes called combining like terms.

Like terms are terms that have the same variable part; in our expression, x and $3x$ are like terms, and 2 and 6 are like terms. We can combine like terms like this:

$x + 3x + 2 + 6 = 4x + 8$

The terms $4x$ and 8 are not alike, so they cannot be combined. Therefore, the simplest equivalent expression of $x + 2 + 3x + 6$ is $4x + 8$. Let's double-check to make sure the simplified expression is equivalent to our original expression: substituting 5 for x again, we get $4(5) + 8 = 28$ which is the same as the value we found before.

You may have noticed that both of the terms in our simplified expression are multiples of 4. This means that we can factor a 4 out of each term to create another equivalent expression. **Factoring** is the same as using the distributive property in reverse. Instead of multiplying a number by all the terms inside a set of parentheses, we divide a number out of all of the terms and write that number outside a set of parentheses, like this:

$4x + 8 = 4(x + 2)$

Let's check again to make sure the expressions are equivalent. The value of our factored expression when x is equal to 5 is $4(5 + 2) = 4(7) = 28$ again.

Let's try a more complicated example: $4(2x + 2) + 3 + 4x$. When we examine this expression, we notice that there is a term inside a set of parentheses, $4(2x + 2)$. This means that there are 4 groups of $(2x + 2)$, or more specifically that there are 4 groups of $2x$ and 4 groups of 2. We can use the distributive property to expand this term, then apply the commutative property to reorder all the terms, and finally combine like terms to write an equivalent expression, like this:

$4(2x + 2) + 3 + 4x$
$= 4(2x) + 4(2) + 3 + 4x$
$= 8x + 8 + 3 + 4x$
$= 8x + 4x + 8 + 3$
$= 12x + 11$

As before, we can check that our simplified expression is equivalent to the original expression by choosing a value for x, such as 5, and making sure the two expressions name the same number. Just don't forget to follow the correct order of operations.

$4(2x + 2) + 3 + 4x \longrightarrow 4(2(5) + 2) + 3 + 4(5) = 4(10 + 2) + 3 + 20 = 4(12) + 23 = 48 + 23 = 71$

$12x + 11 \longrightarrow 12(5) + 11 = 60 + 11 = 71$

Note: As a general rule, you shouldn't choose 0 or 1 for the value of x, because these two numbers have special properties that may lead to equal values even when the expressions are not equivalent.

As long as you are careful, writing equivalent expressions usually involves the very same operations that your child has been using since they learned to add, subtract, multiply, and divide. Sometimes, however, students make careless errors, especially when working with signed numbers. For example, writing an equivalent expression for $10y - 4(2y + 1)$ involves just a few basic operations, but is very often answered incorrectly due to a careless error. Why do you think this is true? If you answered "because of the minus sign in front of the 4," then you are exactly right! Here's what the **wrong** answer looks like:

$$10y - 4(2y + 1) = 10y - 8y + 4 = 2y + 4$$

To avoid this type of error, encourage your child to always write out the terms when they apply the distributive property. Here's what the correct answer looks like:

$$10y - 4(2y + 1) = 10y - 4(2y) - 4(1) = 10y - 8y - 4 = 2y - 4$$

It's just one extra step, and is well worth it!

Now, what if the coefficients of the terms in the expressions are not whole numbers? They could also be fractions or decimals. An example follows. Notice that the steps are the same as before: apply the distributive property, apply the commutative property, and combine like terms.

$$2x + \frac{1}{2}(5 + 6x) + \frac{3}{2}$$
$$= 2x + \frac{1}{2}(5) + \frac{1}{2}(6x) + \frac{3}{2}$$
$$= 2x + \frac{5}{2} + 3x + \frac{3}{2}$$
$$= 2x + 3x + \frac{5}{2} + \frac{3}{2}$$
$$= 5x + \frac{8}{2}$$
$$= 5x + 4$$

The calculations are a bit messier, but the process is exactly the same. Now, let's practice identifying and writing equivalent expressions.

? Quiz

1. Which expression is equivalent to $6x + 7 - 2(2x + 3)$?
    A. $2x + 1$ B. $2x + 4$ C. $2x + 10$ D. $2x + 13$

2. For what value(s) of x do the expressions $2x + 3x + 4x$ and $9x$ yield the same result?
    A. 0 B. 1 C. 0 and 1 D. All numbers

3. Which expression is equivalent to $3(x + \frac{1}{3}) + 4 - \frac{3}{4}(8x - 4)$?

    A. $-23x + 8$ B. $-21x + 1$ C. $-3x + 1$ D. $-3x + 8$

4. Are $3x - 2 + 4(x + 1)$ and $7x + 2$ equivalent expressions? Justify your answer.

5. Are $0.3x + 0.5(x + 3) + 2$ and $0.3(x + 10) + 0.5x + 2$ equivalent expressions? Justify your answer.

 Answers

1. Which expression is equivalent to $6x + 7 - 2(2x + 3)$?
    A. $2x + 1$ B. $2x + 4$ C. $2x + 10$ D. $2x + 13$

    The correct answer is A:
    $6x + 7 - 2(2x + 3)$
    $= 6x + 7 - 2(2x) - 2(3)$
    $= 6x + 7 - 4x - 6$
    $= 6x - 4x + 7 - 6$
    $= 2x + 1$

    This question requires your child to apply the distributive property, the commutative property, and to combine like terms to find an expression that is equivalent to a given expression. The question addresses standard 6.EE.A.3.

2. For what value(s) of x do the expressions $2x + 3x + 4x$ and $9x$ yield the same result?

   A. 0   B. 1   C. 0 and 1   D. All numbers

   The correct answer is D: The expressions are equivalent so no matter what value of x you choose, the two expressions will yield the same result.

   This question assesses your child's understanding of what it means for two expressions to be equivalent. The question addresses standard 6.EE.A.4.

3. Which expression is equivalent to $3(x + \frac{1}{3}) + 4 - \frac{3}{4}(8x - 4)$?

   A. $-23x + 8$ B. $-21x + 1$ C. $-3x + 1$ D. $-3x + 8$

   The correct answer is D:

   $$3(x + \frac{1}{3}) + 4 - \frac{3}{4}(8x - 4)$$

   $$= 3(x) + 3(\frac{1}{3}) + 4 - \frac{3}{4}(8x) - \frac{3}{4}(-4)$$

   $$= 3x + 1 + 4 - 6x + 3$$
   $$= 3x - 6x + 1 + 4 + 3$$
   $$= -3x + 8$$

   This question requires your child to apply the distributive property, the commutative property, and to combine like terms to find an expression that is equivalent to a given expression. The question addresses standard 6.EE.A.3.

4. Are $3x - 2 + 4(x + 1)$ and $7x + 2$ equivalent expressions? Justify your answer.

   The correct answer is Yes. $3x - 2 + 4(x + 1)$ simplifies to $7x + 2$:
   $3x - 2 + 4(x + 1)$
   $= 3x - 2 + 4(x) + 4(1)$
   $= 3x - 2 + 4x + 4$
   $= 3x + 4x - 2 + 4$
   $= 7x + 2$

5. Are $0.3x + 0.5(x + 3) + 2$ and $0.3(x + 10) + 0.5x + 2$ equivalent expressions? Justify your answer.

   The correct answer is No:

$0.3x + 0.5(x + 3) + 2$	$0.3(x + 10) + 0.5x + 2$
$= 0.3x + 0.5(x) + 0.5(3) + 2$	$= 0.3(x) + 0.3(10) + 0.5x + 2$
$= 0.3x + 0.5x + 1.5 + 2$	$= 0.3x + 3 + 0.5x + 2$
$= 0.8x + 3.5$	$= 0.3x + 0.5x + 3 + 2$
	$= 0.8x + 5$

The constant terms, 3.5 and 5, are not equivalent so the expressions are not equivalent.

Questions 4 and 5 require your child to identify whether two expressions are equivalent. The questions address standard 6.EE.A.4.

THE STANDARD

CCSS.Math.Content.6.EE.B.7: Solve real-world and mathematical problems by writing and solving equations of the form x + p = q and px = q for cases in which p, q and x are all non-negative rational numbers.

What does it mean?

This mathematics standard focuses on solving equations. An equation is nothing more than a statement that two expressions are equal. Your child will apply the properties of operations that they used to write equivalent expressions in the previous lesson, and they will use inverse operations to isolate the variable and solve for its value. Equation solving skills are essential for algebra, higher mathematics, and science.

Try this together

An **equation** is a statement that two expressions are equal, one on each side of the equal sign. Sometimes, to solve an equation, you can simply think of a number that makes the statement true. Ask yourself this: If $x + 5 = 20$, what is x? You probably know that $15 + 5 = 20$, so x must equal 15.

Unfortunately, it's not always that simple, so we need a strategy for solving equations. The general process (strategy) for solving an equation is to **isolate the variable** (get it by itself) on one side of the equal sign. To do this, you can use inverse operations to "undo" anything that has been done to the variable (addition and subtraction are inverse operations, and multiplication and division are inverse operations).

Let's look at our example from before: $x + 5 = 20$. Notice that in the equation, 5 has been added to x. Subtraction is the inverse of addition, so we can subtract 5 from the left side of the equation to get x by itself. To keep the equation balanced, we must also subtract 5 from the right side of the equation.

$$x + 5 = 20$$
$$x + 5 - 5 = 20 - 5$$
$$x = 15$$

We now have the solution, $x = 15$. We can check our answer by substituting 15 for x in the original equation: $15 + 5 = 20$ is a true statement, so the solution is correct.

Let's try a slightly harder example. Suppose we want to solve for x in the equation $\frac{x}{4} = 20$.

Notice that 4 divides evenly into 20. This actually leads to a common wrong answer, $x = 5$. Encourage your child to take the time to think about the inverse operation that is needed here—in the equation, x is being *divided* by 4, so the inverse operation is *multiplication*:

$$\frac{x}{4} = 20$$
$$4 \cdot \frac{x}{4} = 4 \cdot 20$$
$$x = 80$$

The solution is $x = 80$. Your child can also avoid careless errors by always checking their answer: $\frac{80}{4}$ does equal 20, so the solution is correct.

Lots of real-world scenarios can be represented by equations. Let's look at a common application.

> Suppose the sales tax in a particular state is 7%. Mathematically, this means that the tax is 0.07 times the cost of the item. If the sales tax on a pair of roller skates is $4.20, what is the pre-tax cost of the roller skates?

To solve the problem, let's start by writing an equation to represent the situation. In words, the equation might look like 0.07 *times* the cost of the roller skates *equals* the amount of the tax. If we let c represent the pre-tax cost of the roller skates, the equation is $0.07c = 4.20$. (You can use x for the variable if you like, but sometimes using a letter that matches the words in the problem helps students make sense of the equation.)

Now, we need to solve for c. Let's use inverse operations. In the equation, c is being multiplied by 0.07, so we need to divide both sides of the equation by 0.07, like this:

$$0.07c = 4.20$$
$$\frac{0.07c}{0.07} = \frac{4.20}{0.07}$$
$$c = 60$$

Don't forget to check the answer: $0.07(60) = 4.20$ so the solution is correct.

Here's a tip about decimals: to make the numbers easier to work with, you can move the decimal point as many times as you like, as long as you move it the same number of places for all terms on both sides of the equation. This creates equivalent expressions, so the solutions will also be equivalent. To solve the previous problem, we could start by moving the decimal point two places to the right, in both terms.

$$0.07c = 4.20$$
$$7c = 420$$
$$\frac{7c}{7} = \frac{420}{7}$$
$$c = 60$$

 Quiz

1. What is the value of x in the equation $x + 16 = 28$?
   A. −12   B. 12   C. 16   D. 44

2. Solve the equation below for x.

   $$\frac{1}{5}x = 25$$

   A. 5   B. 20   C. 30   D. 125

3. A company charges a shipping fee for purchasing a soccer ball online. The cost of the soccer ball is $10.00 and the total bill is $12.50. If the variable f represents the shipping fee, which equation could you solve to find the amount of the fee?
   A. $10f = 12.50$ B. $12.50f = 10$
   C. $f - 10 = 12.50$ D. $f + 10 = 12.50$

4. What value of x makes the equation $1.2x = 48$ true? Explain your answer.

5. Solve the equation $t + \frac{1}{2} = 6$ for t. Write your answer as a whole number, a proper fraction, or a mixed number.

 **Answers**

1. What is the value of *x* in the equation *x* + 16 = 28?

   A. −12   B. 12   C. 16   D. 44

   The correct answer is B. Use inverse operations to find the value of x. In the equation, 16 has been added to x, so subtract 16 from both sides of the equation:

   $$x + 16 = 28$$

   $$x + 16 - 16 = 28 - 16$$

   $$x = 12$$

2. Solve the equation below for *x*.

   $$\frac{1}{5}x = 25$$

   A. 5   B. 20   C. 30   D. 125

   The correct answer is D. Use inverse operations to solve for x. In the equation, x is being multiplied by $\frac{1}{5}$, so you need to divide both sides of the equation by $\frac{1}{5}$. This is the same as multiplying by the reciprocal of $\frac{1}{5}$, which is 5.

   $$\frac{1}{5}x = 25$$

   $$5\left(\frac{x}{5}\right) = (25)5$$

   $$\cancel{5}\left(\frac{x}{\cancel{5}}\right) = (25)5$$

   $$x = 125$$

   Questions 1 and 2 require your child to solve equations of the form x + p = q and px = q. These questions address standard 6.EE.B.7.

3. A company charges a shipping fee for purchasing a soccer ball online. The cost of the soccer ball is $10.00 and the total bill is $12.50. If the variable *f* represents the shipping fee, which equation could you solve to find the amount of the fee?

   A. 10*f* = 12.50   B. 12.50*f* = 10   C. *f* − 10 = 12.50   D. *f* + 10 = 12.50

   The correct answer is D. The cost of the soccer ball, $10, plus the shipping fee, f, is equal to the total cost, $12.50. You can write this as 10 + f = 12.50, or if you apply the commutative property of addition, you can write the equivalent equation, f + 10 = 12.50.

   Question 3 requires your child to write an equation of the form x + p = q where x, p, and q are nonnegative numbers. The question addresses standard 6.EE.B.7.

4. What value of x makes the equation $1.2x = 48$ true? Explain your answer.

    The correct answer is 40. To find the value of x that makes the equation true, use inverse operations to solve the equation for x. The variable is being multiplied by 1.2, so divide both sides of the equation by 1.2. You can also rewrite the equation (by moving the decimal point one place) as 12x = 480 and divide both sides by 12:

    $$1.2x = 48$$
    $$12x = 480$$
    $$\frac{12x}{12} = \frac{480}{12}$$
    $$x = 40$$

5. Solve the equation $t + \frac{1}{2} = 6$ for *t*. Write your answer as a whole number, a proper fraction, or a mixed number.

    The correct answer is $5\frac{1}{2}$. You can use inverse operations to solve the equation, but in this problem it may be easier to think about what value makes the statement true—if you add a $\frac{1}{2}$ to $5\frac{1}{2}$, the result is 6, so t must equal $5\frac{1}{2}$.

    Questions 4 and 5 require your child to solve equations of the form x + p = q and px = q. These questions address standard 6.EE.B.7.

THE STANDARDS

CCSS.Math.Content.6.EE.B.5: Understand solving an equation or inequality as a process of answering a question: which values from a specified set, if any, make the equation true? Use **substitution** to determine whether a given number in a specified set makes an equation or inequality true.

CCSS.Math.Content.6.EE.B.6: Use variables to represent numbers and write expressions when solving a real-world or mathematical problem; understand that a variable can represent an unknown number, or, depending on the purpose at hand, any number in a specified set.

CCSS.Math.Content.6.EE.B.7: Solve real-world and mathematical problems by writing and solving equations of the form $x + p = q$ and $px = q$ for cases in which p, q and x are all non-negative rational numbers.

What does it mean?

These mathematics standards focus on writing and solving equations. Specifically, standard 6.EE.B.5 focuses on solving equations by substitution from a specified set of values. This skill is important, as it is sometimes more efficient to check a possible solution than to solve the equation using inverse operations (when the equation is extremely difficult to solve). Standard 6.EE.B.6 focuses on using variables and numbers to write an equation that represents a real-world scenario, and then to solve the equation. Let's take a look.

Try this together

In the previous lesson, your child learned to use inverse operations to solve some basic equations. In this lesson, the emphasis is on solving real-world problems by writing equations and by using substitution to solve the equations. **Substitution** simply means replacing the variable in the equation with a specific value to determine whether or not it makes the equation true. Let's give this problem a try:

A child enters an archery contest. Each child shoots 5 arrows. The target consists of a yellow circle in the center (10 points) surrounded by concentric circles that form rings around the yellow center: red (7 points), blue (5 points), black (3 points), and white (1 point).

Kayla's first 3 arrows all land in the same colored ring. Her other 2 arrows add up to 15 points. Her total score is 36 points. Into which colored ring did her first 3 arrows land?

Some students panic when they see word problems like this. The question does sound complicated, but if you work it out one step at a time, it is not as difficult as it may seem. Let's start by writing a mathematical sentence that represents Kayla's score:

3 shots *times* some number of points *plus* 2 shots that total 15 points *equals* total score, 36

Now, we need to translate the sentence into numbers, letters, and symbols. Again, focus on one part of the sentence at a time. Pick a variable, like *s*, to represent the number of points assigned to the ring in which Kayla's first 3 shots landed.

3 shots *times* some number of points *plus* 2 shots that total 15 points *equals* total score, 36
$$3s \qquad + \qquad 15 \qquad = \qquad 36$$

So, our equation is $3s + 15 = 36$. Based on the information given in the problem, the only possible values for *s* are the points assigned to each ring (1, 3, 5, 7, or 10). We can solve for *s* by substituting each possible value into the equation to see which one makes it true.

$3s + 15 = 36$				
$s = 1$: $3(1) + 15 = 36$ $3 + 15 = 36$ $18 \neq 36$ so $s \neq 1$	$s = 3$: $3(3) + 15 = 36$ $9 + 15 = 36$ $24 \neq 36$ so $s \neq 3$	$s = 5$: $3(5) + 15 = 36$ $15 + 15 = 36$ $30 \neq 36$ so $s \neq 5$	$s = 7$: $3(7) + 15 = 36$ $21 + 15 = 36$ $36 = 36$ so $s = 7$	$s = 10$: $3(10) + 15 = 36$ $30 + 15 = 36$ $45 \neq 36$ so $s \neq 10$

The only value of *s* that makes the equation true is $s = 7$, so Kayla's first 3 arrows landed in the ring that has a value of 7 points, which is the red ring.

Try these skills on the quiz below. While working through these problems, encourage your child to first write a mathematical sentence in words, then assign a variable to represent the unknown amount, and finally, translate the sentence to numbers, letters, and symbols.

❓ Quiz

1. Three boys in Jeremy's class are 2 inches taller than Jeremy. Together, the heights of the three taller boys total 150 inches. If *h* represents Jeremy's height, which equation shows the information given about the three boys?
   A. $3h = 150$ B. $3h + 2 = 150$ C. $h + 2 = 150$ D. $3(h + 2) = 150$

2. In a bag, there are 5 identical pieces of candy. An empty bag weighs 10 grams. The total weight of the bag of candy is 22.5 grams. There are 3 possible types of candy that could be in the bag. Mints weigh 2.5 grams each, gummy bears weigh 5 grams each, and fudge weighs 7.5 grams per piece. Which kind of candy is in the bag? Justify your

answer by writing and solving an equation. Use the variable *w* to represent the weight of the candy.

3. The total volume of a car's gas tank is 18 gallons. Sarah's dad completely fills the tank with 11 gallons. How much gas was initially in the tank?
   A. 0 gallons   B. 7 gallons   C. 11 gallons   D. 18 gallons

4. There are 12 identical drink cans plus a bonus can in a carton. The drinks could be juice (8 oz. cans), energy drink (10 oz. cans), water (12 oz. cans), or soda (16 oz. cans). The total fluid volume of the liquid in the carton is 156 ounces. What kind of drink is in the cans?
   A. soda   B. juice   C. water   D. energy drink

5. Four children went bowling. One child scored 56 points, while another scored 39 points. The other two children had identical scores. The total score in the game was 193 points. Which of the equations below is the SIMPLEST equation to describe this situation?
   A. $2x + 193 = 95$ B. $2x + 95 = 193$
   C. $x + x + 193 + 39 = 56$ D. $56 + 39 + x + x = 193$

 **Answers**

1. *Three boys in Jeremy's class are 2 inches taller than Jeremy. Together, the heights of the three taller boys total 150 inches. If h represents Jeremy's height, which equation shows the information given about the three boys?*
   A. $3h = 150$ B. $3h + 2 = 150$ C. $h + 2 = 150$ D. $3(h + 2) = 150$
   The correct answer is D. Write a sentence, then translate it into numbers, letters, and symbols, like this:
   3 boys times (Jeremy's height, h, plus 2) is equal to the total inches, 150
   $3(h + 2) = 150$
   Question 1 requires your child to use a variable to represent an unknown amount (Jeremy's height) and to write an equation that represents a real-world scenario. The question addresses standard 6.EE.B.6.

2. *In a bag, there are 5 identical pieces of candy. An empty bag weighs 10 grams. The total weight of the bag of candy is 22.5 grams. There are 3 possible types of candy that could be in the bag. Mints weigh 2.5 grams each, gummy bears weigh 5 grams each, and fudge weighs 7.5 grams per piece. Which kind of candy is in the bag? Justify your*

answer by writing and solving an equation. Use the variable *w* to represent the weight of the candy.

The correct answer is mints. Five times the weight of one piece of candy, w, plus the weight of the bag, 10 grams, is equal to the total weight, 22.5 grams, so you can write the equation as 5w + 10 = 22.5. Now, test each of the possible weights to see which one makes the equation true.

5(2.5) + 10 = 22.5	5(5) + 10 = 22.5	5(7.5) + 10 = 22.5
12.5 + 10 = 22.5	25 + 10 = 22.5	37.5 + 10 = 22.5
22.5 = 22.5 so w = 2.5	35 ≠ 22.5 so w ≠ 5	47.5 ≠ 22.5 so w ≠ 7.5

One piece of the candy weighs 2.5 grams, so the candies are mints.

Question 2 requires your child to write and solve an equation by substitution involving a real-world scenario. The problem addresses standard 6.EE.B.5.

3. The total volume of a car's gas tank is 18 gallons. Sarah's dad completely fills the tank with 11 gallons. How much gas was initially in the tank?

    A. 0 gallons   *B. 7 gallons*   *C. 11 gallons*   *D. 18 gallons*

    The correct answer is B. Let g represent the amount of gas already in the car's tank. Sarah's dad added 11 gallons to reach the total capacity of 18 gallons. The equation is g + 11 = 18. Solve the equation using inverse operations: 11 has been added to g, so subtract 11 from both sides of the equation to isolate g:

    $$g + 11 = 18$$
    $$g + 11 - 11 = 18 - 11$$
    $$g = 7 \text{ gallons}$$

    Question 3 requires your child to solve a real-world problem by writing and solving an equation of the form x + p = q where p, q, and x are nonnegative rational numbers. The question addresses standard 6.EE.B.7.

4. There are 12 identical drink cans plus a bonus can in a carton. The drinks could be juice (8 oz. cans), energy drink (10 oz. cans), water (12 oz. cans), or soda (16 oz. cans). The total fluid volume of the liquid in the carton is 156 ounces. What kind of drink is in the cans?

    A. soda   *B. juice*   *C. water*   *D. energy drink*

    The correct answer is C. There are 12 cans in the carton plus a bonus can for a total of 13 cans. If x represents the number of ounces in one can, then 13 times x, or 13x, is equal to the total volume, 156 ounces. So, the equation becomes 13x = 156. You can solve this equation by substituting the possible volumes into the equation, or by using inverse operations. The quicker method in this problem is to use inverse operations.

$$13x = 156$$

$$\frac{13x}{13} = \frac{156}{13}$$

$$x = 12$$

The number of ounces in one can is 12, so the drink must be water.

Question 4 requires your child to write and solve an equation of the form px = q that relates to a real-world scenario. Your child may solve the equation by substitution or by using inverse operations. The question addresses standards 6.EE.B.5 and 6.EE.B.7.

5. Four children went bowling. One child scored 56 points, while another scored 39 points. The other two children had identical scores. The total score in the game was 193 points. Which of the equations below is the SIMPLEST equation to describe this situation?

   A. $2x + 193 = 95$ B. $2x + 95 = 193$

   C. $x + x + 193 + 39 = 56$ D. $56 + 39 + x + x = 193$

   The correct answer is B. If the variable x represents the unknown scores, you could write the equation as 56 + 39 + x + x = 193. Because the problems asks for the SIMPLEST equation, you must then combine like terms to get 95 + 2x = 193. This is the same as 2x + 95 = 193 (by the commutative property of addition).

   Question 5 requires your child to use a variable to represent numbers and to write an equation, in simplest form, that represents a real-world scenario. The question addresses standard 6.EE.B.6.

THE STANDARD

CCSS.Math.Content.6.EE.C.9: Use variables to represent two quantities in a real-world problem that change in relationship to one another; write an equation to express one quantity, thought of as the dependent variable, in terms of the other quantity, thought of as the independent variable. Analyze the relationship between the dependent and independent variables using graphs and tables, and relate these to the equation. For example, in a problem involving motion at constant speed, list and graph ordered pairs of distances and times, and write the equation d = 65t to represent the relationship between distance and time.

What does it mean?

This mathematics standard focuses on identifying variables in real-world problems as being either independent or dependent, and determining the relationships between the variables. The relationship may be presented using a verbal description, in a table of values, or on a graph. The standard also focuses on using the relationship between the variables to write an equation that represents the situation. These skills are essential not only for math, but also for science, business, and economics. Let's see.

Try this together

Jim conducts an experiment for a science fair project. In the experiment, he starts with a bean plant that has a height of 10 cm. He regularly waters and fertilizes the plant for 6 weeks. On Friday morning of each week, he measures the height of the plant and records the height in the table below.

Time (weeks)	0	1	2	3	4	5	6
Height (cm)	10	12	14	16	18	20	22

Jim wants to display the data on a graph and to write an equation that represents the plant's height during the 6-week period. To do this, he needs to:

1. Identify which variable (time or height) is the dependent variable and which is the independent variable. This will help Jim label his graph. The horizontal axis on a graph always represents the independent variable and the vertical axis represents the dependent variable.

2. Plot the data using coordinate points in the form (independent variable, dependent variable).

3. Determine the pattern (using the graph or the table) from one point to the next and write the equation using the initial height and the pattern. As a general rule, the dependent variable should be written by itself on the left side of the equal sign.

Let's help Jim out by completing one task at a time.

1. The height of the plant *depends* on the amount of time that has passed, so height is the dependent variable and time is the independent variable. This means that Jim should label the horizontal axis "Time (in weeks)" and the vertical axis "Height (cm)".
2. Then, he should plot the data as coordinate points in the form (time, height). Here's what his graph might look like:

Height of a Bean Plant

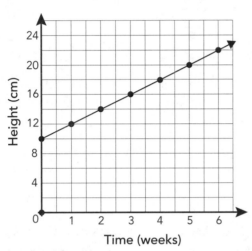

Notice that the data points form a straight line. This means that the bean plant is growing at a constant rate, which is good news because it also means there is a pattern that we can find to write the equation.

3. To find the pattern, let's look back at the table and then we'll compare it to our graph.

Time (weeks)	0	1	2	3	4	5	6
Height (cm)	10	12	14	16	18	20	22

+2 +2 +2 +2 +2 +2

Notice that for each additional week that goes by, the height increases by 2 cm. This tells us that the **unit rate** is 2 cm per week. We can use this information to write our equation. Also, notice that at time = 0 weeks, the height of the bean plant was 10 cm. This is called the **initial height** and will be important to writing the equation as well. As in Chapter J, let's write a mathematical sentence (in words) first. The height of the plant, *h*, is equal to its initial height, 10 cm, plus the amount it grows per week, 2 cm, times the number of weeks, *w*, that pass. The equation is

$h = 10 + 2w$.

We can check our equation using a few points from the graph, for example (0, 10), (2, 14), and (6, 22). If the equation is correct, the points will make it true.

$h = 10 + 2w$ $\quad\quad$ $10 = 10 + 2(0)$ $\quad$ $14 = 10 + 2(2)$ $\quad$ $22 = 10 + 2(6)$

$\quad\quad\quad\quad\quad\quad\quad\quad\quad\quad$ $10 = 10$ $\quad\quad\quad\quad$ $14 = 14$ $\quad\quad\quad\quad$ $22 = 22$

All the points match the equation, so it is correct. As a general rule, when points form a straight line, the equation looks like: dependent variable = unit rate · independent variable + starting amount. If the graph starts at the origin (0, 0), the equation looks like: dependent variable = unit rate · independent variable.

❓ Quiz

Use this passage to answer questions 1-2.

> A clerk puts an empty bag on a scale and weighs it at 1 ounce. She begins filling the bag with coffee beans, one cup at a time. After each cup, she measures the weight of the bag of coffee. With each cup, the weight increases by 12 ounces.

1. In this situation, what is the independent variable? What is the dependent variable?

2. If c represents the number of cups of coffee and w represents the weight of the bag of coffee, which of the following equations describes the relationship between c and w?
   A. $c = 12w + 1$ $\quad$ B. $w = 12c + 1$ $\quad$ C. $c = w + 13$ $\quad$ D. $w = c + 13$

3. Jill's running coach films her as she runs at a constant speed along a track. From the film, he can determine how far she ran each second. The data are shown in the graph.

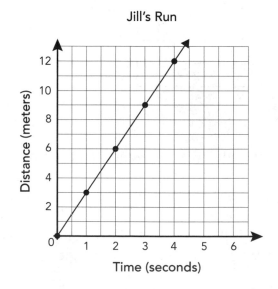

Jill's Run

If *d* represents the distance that Jill runs and *t* represents the number of seconds she runs, which equation shows the relationship between the variables?

A. $t = 3d$ B. $t = d + 3$ C. $d = 3t$ D. $d = t + 3$

The data in the table shows the cost of plastic pipe for various lengths of pipe. Use the data to answer questions 4-5.

Pipe length (feet)	Cost (dollars)
0	0
1	1.25
2	2.50
3	3.75
4	5.00
5	6.25

4. What is the independent variable? What is the dependent variable?

5. Write an equation that shows the relationship between the length, *L*, of the pipe and the cost, *c*.

Answers

Use this passage to answer questions 1-2.

A clerk puts an empty bag on a scale and weighs it at 1 ounce. She begins filling the bag with coffee beans, one cup at a time. After each cup, she measures the weight of the bag of coffee. With each cup, the weight increases by 12 ounces.

1. In this situation, what is the independent variable? What is the dependent variable?

   The correct answer is that the independent variable is the number of cups of coffee beans and the dependent variable is the weight of the bag of coffee. This is because the weight depends on the number of cups placed in the bag.

2. If *c* represents the number of cups of coffee and *w* represents the weight of the bag of coffee, which of the following equations describes the relationship between *c* and *w*?

   A. $c = 12w + 1$ B. $w = 12c + 1$ C. $c = w + 13$ D. $w = c + 13$

   The correct answer is B. The weight, w, of the bag of coffee is the dependent variable so it should be written by itself on one side of the equal sign. The weight of the bag of coffee increases 12 ounces per cup, so the unit rate is 12 and one term on the other side of the equals should be 12 times the number of cups, or 12c. The starting amount is the weight of the empty bag, 1 ounce, so the equation is w = 12c + 1.

   Questions 1 and 2 require your child to identify the variables in a real-world scenario as being dependent or independent, to analyze the relationship between the variables, and to write an equation that shows the relationship. The questions address standard 6.EE.C.9.

3. Jill's running coach films her as she runs at a constant speed along a track. From the film, he can determine how far she ran each second. The data are shown in the graph.

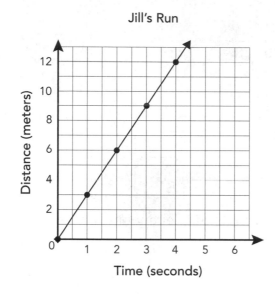

Jill's Run

If *d* represents the distance that Jill runs and *t* represents the number of seconds she runs, which equation shows the relationship between the variables?

A. $t = 3d$ B. $t = d + 3$ C. $d = 3t$ D. $d = t + 3$

The correct answer is C. The distance, d, is graphed on the vertical axis and is therefore the dependent variable and should be written by itself on one side of the equal sign. By looking at the coordinates of the points, you can see that for every second, the distance increases by 3 m, so the unit rate is 3. The starting distance is 0 because at time = 0 seconds, Jill has run 0 meters, so the equation is d = 3t.

Question 3 requires your child to analyze the relationship between the independent and dependent variables shown on a graph and write an equation that shows the relationship between the variables. The question addresses standard 6.EE.C.9.

The data in the table shows the cost of plastic pipe for various lengths of pipe. Use the data to answer questions 4-5.

Pipe length (feet)	Cost (dollars)
0	0
1	1.25
2	2.50
3	3.75
4	5.00
5	6.25

4. What is the independent variable? What is the dependent variable?

   The correct answer is that length is the independent variable and cost is the dependent variable. This is because the cost depends on how long the pipe is.

5. Write an equation that shows the relationship between the length, L, of the pipe and the cost, c.

   The cost, c, is the dependent variable and should be written by itself on one side of the equal sign. From the data in the table, you can see that, for every increase of 1 foot in length, the cost of the pipe increases by $1.25 so the unit rate is 1.25. The starting amount is 0 because 0 feet of pipe will cost $0, so the equation is $c = 1.25L$.

   Questions 4 and 5 require your child to identify the variables in a real-world scenario as being dependent or independent, to analyze the relationship between the variables based on information given in a table, and to write an equation that shows the relationship. The questions address standard 6.EE.C.9.

English Language Arts Post-Test

The following questions are intended to assess your child's reading and writing skills. As with the pre-test, there are a variety of question types at various levels of cognition. These are typical of the types of questions that your sixth grader might experience in the classroom, as homework, and in assessment situations. These items are **not** designed to replicate standardized tests used to assess a child's reading level or a school's progress in helping the child achieve grade level.

A grid at the end provides the main Common Core standard assessed, as well as a brief explanation of the correct answers. This is intended to help you consider how your child is doing in reading and writing after you have presented the lessons in this book. Keep in mind, however, that building reading and writing skills is an ongoing process. The best way to build these skills is to continue to read and write. If the post-test identifies areas in which your child needs improvement, review the strategies in the lessons and continue to focus on these areas when you read with your child.

For each section, read the passage and then answer the questions that follow.

 ## The Man Behind the Golden Gate Bridge

When the Golden Gate Bridge in San Francisco opened on May 27, 1937, there was a great celebration. Thousands of people crossed the bridge that day. Some ran across, while others crossed on stilts or roller skates. One person actually walked across the bridge backwards! No cars were allowed to cross until the next morning.

Among those celebrating was the chief engineer of the bridge. His name was Joseph Baermann Strauss. Strauss couldn't believe that the bridge was finished. Sometimes he didn't think it would ever happen, and that is why he named the poem he wrote when the bridge was completed "The Mighty Work Is Done."

When Strauss was a boy, he never thought about building bridges. Born in Cincinnati, Ohio in 1870, both of his parents were artists. He thought he would become an artist, too. He enjoyed writing poetry, but then something happened that changed his life.

Strauss entered the University of Cincinnati. He wasn't very big, but he tried out for the school's football team. He was hurt during practice and ended up in the school infirmary, which is like a small hospital at a university. He spent his time there looking out the window. What he saw was the first long-span suspension bridge. It was the Cincinnati-Covington Bridge. He became fascinated with bridges.

After he graduated from college in 1892, he worked as a draftsman for the New Jersey Steel and Iron Company. Then he worked for the Lassig Bridge and Iron Works Company in Chicago. Seven years later, Strauss became the main assistant engineer in the firm of Ralph Modjeski, who was a Chicago engineer.

While working for Modjeski, Strauss developed a unique design for drawbridges. Eventually, Strauss started his own drawbridge company in 1904. He built 400 drawbridges across the United States, but that wasn't enough in his mind. He said he wanted to build "the biggest thing of its kind that a man could build."

Then the mayor of San Francisco asked him to help with the plan to build a bridge spanning the Golden Gate. Strauss was ecstatic about the project and knew at once that he had to be part of it. Many people were against the bridge because they didn't think it was necessary. It took a very long time, but finally Strauss and the mayor convinced the public it needed to be done.

Four and a half years later, the bridge was finally built. This suspension bridge was the longest one ever built. It was an engineering marvel and beautiful to look at, too. People were impressed beyond words.

Joseph Strauss had seen the Golden Gate project through to completion, but it had exhausted him and he became ill. He died just one year after the bridge was finished. In his honor, a statue was built of him, which stands on the San Francisco side of the bridge.

1. Which sentence best states the central idea of the passage?
   A. *After the Golden Gate Bridge was finished, its engineer got sick and died.*
   B. *Joseph Strauss was an engineer whose greatest project was designing the Golden Gate Bridge.*
   C. *Joseph Strauss wanted to play football but got hurt and had to stay in the university's infirmary.*
   D. *When the Golden Gate Bridge in San Francisco opened on May 27, 1937, there was a great celebration with thousands of people.*

2. Why did so many people come to the opening of the Golden Gate Bridge?
   A. *They were invited by Joseph Strauss.*
   B. *They were against the building of the bridge.*
   C. *They thought the bridge was going to fall down.*
   D. *They wanted to be among the first to cross the bridge.*

3. Based on its usage in the seventh paragraph, which of the following is closest in meaning to the word *ecstatic*?
   A. *worried*   B. *uncertain*   C. *thrilled*   D. *content*

4. Which detail from the passage supports the statement that building the Golden Gate Bridge for Joseph Strauss was a huge undertaking?
   A. *"What he saw was the first long-span suspension bridge."*
   B. *"After he graduated from college in 1892, he worked as a draftsman for the New Jersey Steel and Iron Company."*
   C. *"Many people were against the bridge."*
   D. *"That is why he named the poem he wrote when the bridge was completed 'The Mighty Work Is Done.'"*

5. What detail from the passage best supports the author's claim that "people were impressed beyond words" by Strauss' achievement?

    A. "He said he wanted to build 'the biggest thing of its kind that a man could build.'"

    B. "In his honor, a statue was built of him, which stands on the San Francisco side of the bridge."

    C. "Strauss couldn't believe that the bridge was finished."

    D. "This suspension bridge was the longest one ever built."

6. Based on its usage in the next-to-last paragraph, which of the following is closest in meaning to the word *marvel*?

    A. decision   B. difficulty   C. nightmare   D. wonder

7. How did being hurt while playing football affect Strauss' life? Use details from the passage in your answer.

    _____

    _____

    _____

 Excerpt from *The Adventures of Tom Sawyer* by Mark Twain

"TOM!"

No answer.

"TOM!"

No answer.

"What's gone with that boy, I wonder? You TOM!"

No answer.

The old lady pulled her spectacles down and looked over them about the room; then she put them up and looked out under them. She seldom or never looked *through* them for so small a thing as a boy; they were her state pair, the pride of her heart, and were built for "style," not service—she could have seen through a pair of stove-lids just as well. She looked perplexed for a moment, and then said, not fiercely, but still loud enough for the furniture to hear:

"Well, I lay if I get hold of you I'll -- "

She did not finish, for by this time she was bending down and punching under the bed with the broom, and so she needed breath to punctuate the punches with. She resurrected nothing but the cat.

"I never did see the beat of that boy!"

She went to the open door and stood in it and looked out among the tomato vines and "jimpson" weeds that constituted the garden. No Tom. So she lifted up her voice at an angle calculated for distance and shouted:

"Y-o-u-u *Tom!*"

There was a slight noise behind her and she turned just in time to seize a small boy by the slack of his roundabout and arrest his flight.

"There! I might 'a' thought of that closet. What you been doing in there?"

"Nothing."

"Nothing! Look at your hands. And look at your mouth. What *is* that truck?"

"*I* don't know, aunt."

"Well, *I* know. It's jam -- that's what it is. Forty times I've said if you didn't let that jam alone I'd skin you. Hand me that switch."

The switch hovered in the air—the peril was desperate—

"My! Look behind you, aunt!"

The old lady whirled round, and snatched her skirts out of danger. The lad fled on the instant, scrambled up the high board-fence, and disappeared over it.

His aunt Polly stood surprised a moment, and then broke into a gentle laugh.

"Hang the boy, can't I never learn anything? Ain't he played me tricks enough like that for me to be looking out for him by this time? But old fools is the biggest fools there is. Can't learn an old dog new tricks, as the saying is. But my goodness, he never plays them alike, two days, and how is a body to know what's coming? He 'pears to know just how long he can torment me before I get my dander up, and he knows if he can make out to put me off for a minute or make me laugh, it's all down again and I can't hit him a lick. I ain't doing my duty by that boy, and that's the Lord's truth, goodness knows. Spare the rod and spile the child, as the Good Book says. I'm a laying up sin and suffering for us both, *I* know. He's full of the Old Scratch, but laws-a-me! he's my own dead sister's boy, poor thing, and I ain't got the heart to lash him, somehow. Every time I let him off, my conscience does hurt me so, and every time I hit him my old heart most breaks."

8. Write a brief summary of the important events in this passage.

_____

_____

_____

9. Read the following sentence from the passage: "She went to the open door and stood in it and looked out among the tomato vines and 'jimpson' weeds that constituted the garden." Based on its usage, which of the following is closest in meaning to the word *constituted*?

   A. *formed*   B. *made legal*

   C. *added water*   D. *caused to wither*

10. Why does Tom scare his aunt?
    A. *He wants to get away.*
    B. *He wants to make her laugh.*
    C. *He thinks she needs a scare.*
    D. *He thinks something bad is about to happen.*

11. Which sentence from the passage best describes how Aunt Polly feels about Tom?
    A. *She went to the open door and stood in it and looked out among the tomato vines and weeds in the garden: no Tom there.*
    B. *"'Nothing! Look at your hands and look at your mouth; what IS that stuff?'"*
    C. *"'Ain't he played me tricks enough like that for me to be looking out for him by this time?'"*
    D. *"'Every time I let him off, my conscience does hurt me so, and every time I punish him my old heart most breaks.'"*

12. Based on its usage near the beginning of the passage, which of the following is closest in meaning to the word *perplexed*?

    A. *fatigued*   B. *amused*   C. *puzzled*   D. *annoyed*

13. Why does Aunt Polly break into laughter after Tom runs away? Use details from the story in your answer.

    _____

    _____

    _____

    _____

14. Based on this excerpt, what is your opinion of the boy Tom Sawyer?

    _____

    _____

    _____

    _____

 ## Excerpt from *A Village Singer* by Mary Wilkins Freeman

The church was already filled with this soft sylvan music—the tender harmony of the leaves and the south wind, and the sweet, desultory whistles of birds—when the choir arose and began to sing.

In the center of the row of women singers stood Alma Way. All the people stared at her, and turned their ears critically. She was the new leading soprano. Candace Whitcomb, the old one, who had sung in the choir for forty years, had lately been given her dismissal. The audience considered that her voice had grown too cracked and uncertain on the upper notes. There had been much complaint, and after long deliberation the church officers had made known their decision as mildly as possible to the old singer. She had sung for the last time the Sunday before, and Alma Way had been engaged to take her place. With the exception of the organist, the leading soprano was the only paid musician in the large choir. The salary was very modest; still, the village people considered it large for a young woman. Alma was from the adjoining village of East Derby; she had quite a local reputation as a singer.

Now she fixed her large solemn blue eyes; her long, delicate face, which had been pretty, turned paler; the blue flowers on her bonnet trembled; her little thin gloved hands, clutching the singing book, shook perceptibly; but she sang out bravely. The most formidable mountain height of the world, self-distrust and timidity, arose before her, but her nerves were braced for its ascent. In the midst of the hymn she had a solo; her voice rang out piercingly sweet; the people nodded admiringly at one another. But suddenly there was a stir; all the faces turned toward the windows on the south side of the church. Above the din of the wind and the birds, above Alma Way's sweetly straining tones, arose another female voice, singing another hymn to another tune.

"It's her," the women whispered to each other; they were half aghast, half smiling.

15. Which sentence from the passage best describes what Candace Whitcomb does to upset Alma Way?

   A. *"Candace Whitcomb, the old one, who had sung in the choir for forty years, had lately been given her dismissal."*

   B. *"The salary was very modest; still, the village people considered it large for a young woman."*

   C. *"In the midst of the hymn she had a solo; her voice rang out piercingly sweet; the people nodded admiringly at one another."*

   D. *"Above the din of the wind and the birds, above Alma Way's sweetly straining tones, arose another female voice, singing another hymn to another tune."*

16. In the first paragraph, what does the author mean when she says that the "church was already filled with this soft sylvan music—the tender harmony of the leaves and the south wind, and the sweet, desultory whistles of birds"?

   A. *The author means that the sound of the wind in the leaves and the bird calls detracted from the chorus.*

   B. *The author means that the sound of the leaves moving in the wind and bird calls were hard to hear over.*

   C. *The author means that the sounds of the leaves moving in the wind and the bird calls was like nature's music.*

   D. *The author means that the sound of the wind in the leaves and the bird calls were nicer than the chorus singing.*

17. How does Alma Way feel about singing in the church?

   A. *She feels she is too good a singer for the position.*

   B. *She is nervous but determined to do a good job.*

   C. *She is confident but careful to take long slow breaths.*

   D. *She worries she is not as good as Candace Whitcomb's.*

18. Based on its usage near the beginning of the passage, which of the following is closest in meaning to the word *deliberation*?

   A. *argument*   B. *money payment*

   C. *criticism*   D. *careful thought*

19. Based on its usage near the beginning of the passage, which of the following is closest in meaning to the word *aghast*?

   A. *horrified*   B. *scared*

   C. *dignified*   D. *angry*

20. Using your own words, write a brief summary of the passage.Use correct grammar, punctuation, spelling, and capitalization.

_____

_____

_____

_____

_____

_____

_____

Read the paragraph and decide on the best answer to fill each blank.

(1) Next Wednesday, I will have to decide if _____ to try out for the band or the choir. (2) My grandma always said that good singing _____. (3) But my mom _____ the idea of me playing an instrument, like my dad did in school. (4) Doing both would take a major commitment of time—time _____ sure I have. (5) Why _____ decisions so hard to make?

21. In sentence 1, which is the best choice to fill the blank?

    A. me going   *B. me was going*   *C. I am going*   *D. I be going*

22. In sentence 2, which is the best choice to fill the blank?

    A. runs in our family   *B. runned in our family*
    C. ran in her family   *D. run in her family*

23. In sentence 3, which is the best choice to fill the blank?

    A. like   *B. likes*   *C. will like*   *D. liking*

24. In sentence 4, which is the best choice to fill the blank?

    A. I aren't   *B. I ain't*   *C. I'm not*   *D. I not*

25. In sentence 5, which is the best choice to fill the blank?

    A. will some   *B. can't some*   *C. is some*   *D. are som*

26. Read this draft of a paragraph. Correct the grammar, punctuation, spelling, and capitalization. Also add a concluding sentence that sums up the argument.

    School should not begin before 9:00 a.m. In so many schools around the country students is standing on corners early in the morning waiting for their busses. In some cases, the Sun has'nt even come up! I doen't think thats safe also, young peopel need his or her sleep. Many have too stay up late doing there homework. How can they be expected to get up at the crack of dawn and be alert enough to learn in theyre clases.

 **Answer Key**

Note: The answers to open-ended, constructed response questions are sample answers. Answers will vary, but look for the main ideas to be included.

Highlight any questions that your child gets wrong. Looking at the wrong answers may help to reveal one or more standards with which your child is struggling. Even if your child has done well on this posttest, reviewing the lessons will help him or her become a better reader and writer.

Passage	Question	Answer	Standard(s)
The Man Behind the Golden Gate Bridge			
	1	B	RI.6.2
	2	D	RI.6.1
	3	C	RI.6.4
	4	D	RI.6.8
	5	B	RI.6.8, RI.6.4
	6	D	RI.6.4
	7	After he was hurt playing football, Strauss had to spend time in the infirmary. The window to his room looked out at the first long-span suspension bridge, which was the Cincinati-Covington Bridge. As a result, he got interested in building bridges and then went into the field. Getting hurt changed his life.	RI.6.1
The Adventures of Tom Sawyer	8	Aunt Polly is calling to her nephew, Tom Sawyer, but he doesn't answer. She looks everywhere for him. Suddenly, Polly catches Tom trying to sneak out of a closet. From his dirty face and hands, it's clear he has broken into the jam. As Polly begins to scold him, Tom tricks her and escapes out the door. Polly is left amused by Tom's trickery but also wondering what to do with the boy.	RL.6.2
	9	A	RL.6.4
	10	A	RL.6.1, RL.6.3
	11	D	RL.6.1
	12	C	RL.6.4
	13	Aunt Polly breaks into laughter because even though Tom fools her all the time, she continues to fall for it. She laughs, too, because she doesn't know what to do about disciplining him since she cares about him.	RL.6.1, RL.6.3
	14	Answers will vary. Accept answers in which opinions are well-supported by details in the passage. Possible answer: Tom is irresponsible and mischievous, but he is also clever in the way he outwits Aunt Polly.	RL.6.1, W.6.1
A Village Singer	15	D	RL.6.3, RL.6.1
	16	C	RL.6.4, RL.6.1
	17	B	RL.6.3, RL.6.1
	18	D	RL.6.4

Passage	Question	Answer	Standard(s)
	19	A	RL.6.4
	20	Candace Whitcomb has been fired as the lead singer in a church and Alma Way has been hired to take her place. It's Alma's first time singing, and she is nervous, and the people in the church seem to like her voice. But then they hear another woman singing, and they realize it is Candace Whitcomb.	RL.6.2
	21	C	W.6.5
	22	A	W.6.5
	23	B	W.6.5
	24	C	W.6.5
	25	D	W.6.5
	26	School should not begin before 9:00 a.m. In so many schools around the country, students are standing on corners early in the morning, waiting for their buses. In some cases, the sun hasn't even come up! I don't think that's safe. Also, young people need their sleep. Many have to stay up late doing their homework. How can they be expected to get up at the crack of dawn and be alert enough to learn in their classes? If schools around the country began no earlier than 9:00 AM, that would make a lot of students much better students!	W.6.5, W.6.1

Mathematics Post-Test

1. A rectangular landing strip at an airport has an area of $\frac{1}{16}$ square mile. If the landing strip is $\frac{3}{4}$ miles long, how wide is it?

   A. $\frac{1}{12}$ B. $\frac{3}{64}$ C. $\frac{11}{16}$ D. $\frac{13}{16}$

2. Tiffany earned $300.00 in one week at the art studio where she works. The studio manager took out $54.00 for taxes. Which percent of Tiffany's salary was taken out for taxes?
   A. 15%   B. 18%   C. 20%   D. 30%

3. Jane buys 3 books online. The second book costs twice as much as the first. The third book costs $5 less than the first. The total cost of the 3 books is $55. Which equation could you solve to find the cost of the first book?
   A. $3b = 55$ B. $2b + 5 = 55$ C. $3b - 5 = 55$ D. $4b - 5 = 55$

4. A restaurant automatically adds 18% gratuity (tip), or 0.18 times the total bill, for parties of 6 or more. The tip on a dinner was $27. Write and solve an equation to find the cost, c, of the dinner, before the tip.

5. Henry can lift three times as much weight as Peter. Together, they can lift a combined weight of 300 pounds. How much weight can Peter lift?
   A. 50 pounds   B. 75 pounds   C. 100 pounds   D. 225 pounds

6. It takes Dennis 15 minutes to paint 2 shutters on his house. If there are 12 shutters, how long will it take him to paint all of them?
   A. 45 minutes   B. 60 minutes   C. 90 minutes   D. 180 minutes

Use the coordinate plane below to answer questions 7–8.

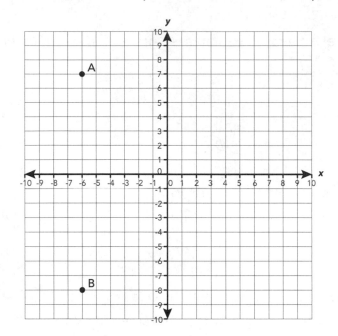

7. What are the coordinates of the two points shown on the coordinate plane?
    A. (–6, 7) and (–6, –8)   B. (7, –6) and (–8, –6)
    C. (–6, 7) and (–8, –6)   D. (7, –6) and (–6, –8)

8. What is the distance between the two points?
    A. 1 unit   B. 7 units   C. 8 units   D. 15 units

9. While making cornbread, Anne uses $\frac{1}{2}$ cup cornmeal for every 2 cups of salted water. If she uses 10 cups of salted water, how much cornmeal should she use?

    A. 1   B. 2.5   C. 3   D. 4.5

10. Lee made $8\frac{1}{2}$ cups of pudding in a mixing bowl. How many $\frac{2}{3}$-cups servings of pudding are in the bowl?

    A. 3   B. $5\frac{2}{3}$ C. 12   D. $12\frac{3}{4}$

11. Annabel's parents limit the amount of television she can watch. For every chapter of a book she reads, she can watch 30 minutes of TV. On Saturday, she reads 5 chapters. How many minutes of TV can she watch that day? Use the table to solve the problem.

Chapters	1	2	3	4	5
Minutes	30				

12. The blade of Don's fencing sword is 35 inches long. He wants to buy a replacement blade, but the supplier's website give the blade lengths in centimeters. There are 2.5 centimeters for every inch. If Don wants to keep the same size blade, how long of a blade, in centimeters, should he order?
    A. 17.5 cm   B. 37.5 cm   C. 87.5 cm   D. 90.0 cm

13. For the equation $4x - 7 = 37$, the possible solutions are 5, 7, 11, and 15. Which is the correct solution?
    A. 5   B. 7   C. 11   D. 15

14. Leona has 6 nonfiction books. This is 30% of all of her books. How many books does she have? Justify your answer using a double number line diagram.

15. Korina is building a fence around her back yard. This table shows the relationship between the length of the fence and the number of nails she will need.

Linear Feet of Fence	Number of Nails
10	120
20	240
30	360
40	480

Let n represent the total number of nails needed and f the length of the fence, in feet. Which equation shows the relationship between n and f?
    A. $f = n + 12$ B. $n = f + 12$ C. $f = 12n$ D. $n = 12f$

16. A clothing store is selling dress shirts at 3 for $36.00 If Mr. Mendoza has $60.00, then how many shirts can he buy?
    A. 3   B. 4   C. 5   D. 6

17. Are $4(2x + 3) + 3(9x - 7)$ and $35x - 9$ equivalent expressions? Justify your answer.

Use the following graph to answer questions 18–19.

A student grows seedlings for an experiment. She measures the height after each day of sunlight. The data are shown in the graph.

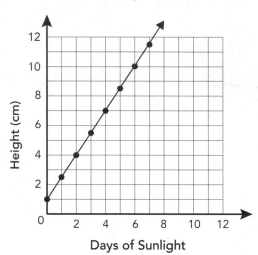

18. What is the independent variable? What is the dependent variable?

19. If d represents the number of days of sunlight and h represents the height of the seedling, which equation shows the relationship between d and h?
    A. $d = 1.5h + 1$ B. $h = 1.5d + 1$ C. $h = d + 1.5$ D. $d = h + 1.5$

20. Which is the solution for the equation $x + 17 = 48$?
    A. 21   B. 31   C. 48   D. 65

21. In a bank deposit, there are 5 rolls of quarters for every 7 roles of dimes. Which is the correct ratio of rolls of quarters to rolls of dimes?
    A. 5:7   B. 5:12   C. 7:5   D. 7:12

22. Which expression is equivalent to $x - \dfrac{2}{3}(9x + 12) - \dfrac{3}{4}(4x + 8)$?

    A. $-10x - 14$ B. $-10x + 20$ C. $-8x - 14$ D. $-8x + 20$

23. What is the solution to the equation below?

$$\frac{2}{5}x = 20$$

A. $x = 8$ B. $x = 12.5$ C. $x = 25$ D. $x = 50$

24. In a shipment of clothing, 8 out of 25 items are dresses. What percent of the shipment is dresses? Justify your answer by drawing a double number line.

25. The middle school Yearbook Club has 21 members. If the ratio of boys to girls is 5 to 2, how many boys are in the club? Draw a tape diagram to support your answer.

 **Answer Key**

Question	Answer	Explanation	Standard
1	A	You can find the area of a rectangle by multiplying the length times the width, $A = l \times w$. If you know the area, you can find one of the dimensions by dividing the area by the other dimension. Here, you know the area and the length, so divide to find the width: $$\frac{1}{16} \div \frac{3}{4} = \frac{1}{16} \times \frac{4}{3} = \frac{1 \times 4}{16 \times 3} = \frac{4}{48} = \frac{1}{12}$$	6.NS.A.1
2	B	You can draw a double number line to solve the problem, like this:	6.RP.A.3b
3	D	Let b represent the price of the first book. Then, the price of the second book is $2b$ and the price of the third book is $b - 5$. The total cost is $55, so you can write the equation $b + 2b + (b - 5) = 55$ and then combine like terms to get $4b - 5 = 55$.	6.EE.B.7

Question	Answer	Explanation	Standard
4	$150	Write the equation in words, then translate it to numbers and symbols: 0.18 times the cost of the dinner equals the tip. The equation is $0.18c = 27$. Then use inverse operations to solve for c.	6.EE.B.7

$$0.18c = 27$$
$$\frac{0.18c}{0.18} = \frac{27}{0.18}$$
$$c = 150$$

Question	Answer	Explanation	Standard
5	B	Let p represent the weight that Peter can lift. Henry can lift 3 times as much, or $3p$, and the total amount they can lift together is 300 pounds, so solve the equation $p + 3p = 300$.	6.EE.B.7

$$p + 3p = 300$$
$$4p = 300$$
$$\frac{4p}{4} = \frac{300}{4}$$
$$p = 75$$

Question	Answer	Explanation	Standard
6	C	This table shows how you can solve the problem using multiplication:	6.RP.A.3b

Shutters	1	2 (2 × 6)
Minutes	15	90 (15 × 6)

Question	Answer	Explanation	Standard
7	A	Point A is 6 units to the left of and 7 units above the origin, so its coordinates are (–6, 7). Point B is 6 units to the left of and 8 units below the origin, so its coordinates are (–6, –8).	6.NS.C.8
8	D	The points have the same x-coordinate, so the distance between them is the absolute value of the difference in their y-coordinates: $|7 - (-8)| = |7 + 8| = |15| = 15$ or $|-8 - 7| = |-15| = 15$.	6.NS.C.8
9	B	Here's how you would solve the problem using a table and multiplication:	6.RP.A.3

Cornmeal (cups)	0.5	2.5 (0.5 × 5)
Salted water (cups)	2	10 (2 × 5)

Question	Answer	Explanation	Standard
10	D	To divide the mixed number by the fraction, first rewrite the mixed number as an improper fraction. Then, to divide one fraction by the other fraction, multiply the first fraction by the reciprocal of the second fraction.	6.NS.A.1

$$8\frac{1}{2} \div \frac{2}{3}$$
$$= \frac{17}{2} \div \frac{2}{3}$$
$$= \frac{17}{2} \cdot \frac{3}{2}$$
$$= \frac{51}{4}$$
$$= 12\frac{3}{4}$$

Question	Answer	Explanation	Standard
11	150 min	Use repeated addition to complete the table—add 30 minutes to each cell in the bottom row.	6.RP.A.3, 6.RP.A.3a

Chapters	1	2	3	4	5
Minutes	30	60	90	120	150

Question	Answer	Explanation	Standard
12	C	This table shows how to solve the problem using multiplication:	6.RP.A.3d

Centimeters	2.5	87.5 (2.5 × 35)
Inches	1	35 (1 × 35)

Question	Answer	Explanation	Standard
13	C	Solve the equation by substituting each of the possible solutions into the equation to see which one makes it true.	6.EE.B.5

4x − 7 − 37			
x = 5: 4(5) − 7 = 37 20 − 7 = 37 13 ≠ 37, so x ≠ 5	x = 7: 4(7) − 7 = 37 28 − 7 = 37 21 ≠ 37, so x ≠ 7	x = 11: 4(11) − 7 = 37 44 − 7 = 37 37 = 37, so x = 11	x = 15: 4(15) − 7 = 37 60 − 7 = 37 53 ≠ 37, so x ≠ 15

Question	Answer	Explanation	Standard
14	20 books	This double number line diagram shows how to arrive at the answer.	6.RP.A.3c

Scale 30% down to 10% percent by dividing by 3; divide 6 by 3 as well to get 2. Then scale 10% up to 100% by multiplying by 10; multiply 2 by 10 as well to get 20 books.

Question	Answer	Explanation	Standard
15	D	To write the equation, look for a pattern in the table. Start with a word equation: the number of nails equals 12 times the number of feet, so the equation is $n = 12f$. Your child can check the answer by substituting each pair of values from the table into the equation: $120 = 12(10)$; $240 = 12(20)$; $360 = 12(30)$; $480 = 12(40)$.	6.EE.C.9

Question	Answer	Explanation	Standard
16	C	You can scale down the given rate to a unit rate and then scale up the unit rate to the desired amount. This double number line shows how:	6.RP.A.3b

Question	Answer	Explanation	Standard
17	Yes		6.EE.A.4

$$4(2x+3)+3(9x-7)$$
$$=4(2x)+4(3)+3(9x)+3(-7)$$
$$=8x+12+27x-21$$
$$=8x+27x+12-21$$
$$=35x-9$$

Question	Answer	Explanation	Standard
18	Independent: days; Dependent: height	The dependent variable is height because it depends on the number of days of sunlight. The independent variable is the number of days of sunlight.	6.EE.C.9
19	B	By looking at the coordinates of the points, you can see that for every day of sunlight, the height of the seedling increases by 1.5 cm, so the unit rate is 1.5. The starting height is 1 because according to the graph, at time = 0 days, the height is 1 cm, so the equation is $h = 1.5d + 1$.	6.EE.C.9
20	B		6.EE.B.7

$$x+17=48$$
$$x+17-17=48-17$$
$$x=31$$

Question	Answer	Explanation	Standard
21	A	This is a part-to-part ratio that compares rolls of quarters (5) to rolls of dimes (7), so the correct ratio is 5:7.	6.RP.A.1
22	C	Apply the distributive property (twice), then apply the commutative property of addition, and finally, combine like terms to simplify the expression:	6.EE.A.3

$$x-\frac{2}{3}\left(\overset{3}{\cancel{9}}x+\overset{4}{\cancel{12}}\right)-\frac{3}{4}\left(\cancel{4}x+\overset{2}{\cancel{8}}\right)$$

$$= x - 2(3x + 4) - 3(x + 2)$$
$$= x - 2(3x) - 2(4) - 3(x) - 3(2)$$
$$= x - 6x - 8 - 3x - 6$$
$$= x - 6x - 3x - 8 - 6$$
$$= -8x - 14$$

Question	Answer	Explanation	Standard
23	D	Use inverse operations to solve for x. In the equation, x is being multiplied by $\frac{2}{5}$, so you need to divide both sides of the equation by $\frac{2}{5}$. This is the same as multiplying by the reciprocal of $\frac{2}{5}$, which is $\frac{5}{2}$. $$x = 20 \div \frac{2}{5} = 20 \cdot \frac{5}{2} = \frac{100}{2} = 50$$	6.EE.B.7
24	32%	The double number line might look like this: 	6.RP.A.3
25	15 boys	You can solve the problem by drawing a tape diagram, like this: There are 7 parts in all, so each part represents 3 members, which means the club has $5 \cdot 3 = 15$ boys.	6.RP.A.3